HALL OF MIRRORS
— SHARDS OF CLARITY

Autism, neuroscience and finding a sense of self

Phoebe Caldwell

Hall Of Mirrors – Shards Of Clarity

Published by:
Pavilion Publishing and Media Ltd
Rayford House
School Road
Hove
East Sussex
BN3 5HX
Tel: 01273 434 943
Fax: 01273 227 308
Email: info@pavpub.com

Published 2017.

A catalogue record for this book is available from the British Library.

ISBN: 978-1-911028-77-2

Pavilion is the leading training and development provider and publisher in the health, social care and allied fields, providing a range of innovative training solutions underpinned by sound research and professional values. We aim to put our customers first, through excellent customer service and value.

Author: Phoebe Caldwell
Production editor: Ruth Chalmers, Pavilion Publishing and Media
Cover design: Anthony Pitt, Pavilion Publishing and Media
Page layout and typesetting: Anthony Pitt, Pavilion Publishing and Media
Printing: CMP Digital Print Solutions

Dedication

Hall of Mirrors – Shards of Clarity is dedicated with gratitude to Donna Williams, who died recently. Much of what I have learned about autism stems from her selfless dedication to teaching the non-autistic world what it feels like to be on the spectrum. She started me off on a journey that has opened up a different world to the one in which I was born and has also taught me about myself.

Apology

This book spans forty-five years of work and I have not always been able to catch up with all the people who have shared their lives with mine. Some have died and some moved on. Where this is so, I have altered their personal details beyond recognition. What remains is the essence of our interactions.

Contents

Foreword

By Professor Kelley Johnson, Professor of Disability, Social Policy Research Centre, UNSW

Our lives are a journey in which we seek constantly to understand each other, reaching out from our subjective worlds constructed through our own unique characteristics and the ways we interpret our lived experience. Sometimes understanding seems to be there, at other times we reach out in vain. In this book Phoebe writes that she aims to 'construct a story'. But the book is also one person's journey to try and understand what the world is like for a group of people who have often found it difficult to understand the world in which they live, and who are often not understood by others.

The journey in this book is one of exploration. Phoebe uses her forty years of working with people labelled as being on the autistic spectrum to consider what life is like for them. But more than this she seeks to use new neuroscientific knowledge to help us understand better how this group of people sees the world. In doing this she includes her own personal experiences, her years of work and most importantly the voices of people labelled as being on the autistic spectrum. This is an unusual synthesis and one which provides the reader with an accessible and interesting account which makes a unique contribution to our understanding of each other.

In trying to understand better how people see the world, Phoebe takes the reader on a personal journey into the recent research which is revealing more about how our brains work to create our own unique perceptions and view of the world. This is not an easy road to walk but her interest and passion inform the pages and provide the reader with an accessible account in which the practical implications of the research are clearly stated.

One of the important consequences of this journey into our inner workings is her view that focusing on the behaviour alone of people labelled as being on the autistic spectrum does not help them to live in a more comfortable world, nor does it help those working with them to better understand what they are experiencing. Phoebe emphasises the importance of recognising and responding to the inner world of people, particularly their emotional responses, in order to communicate better and to change the environment so that it comes closer to matching their needs.

While many books now provide accounts of the lives of people labelled as being on the autistic spectrum, they are often written from one particular perspective. This book is interdisciplinary in its approach. As part of her journey Phoebe draws on history, psychology, neuroscience and personal narratives, bringing them together through her own voice.

As someone who is not a biologist or a neuroscientist but who has worked with people with disabilities for a long time, I was somewhat wary about reading in an area outside my comfort zone. And I wondered as I started the book whether it was going to medicalise people labelled as being on the autistic spectrum. However, while I was challenged by some of the research, I also came to a view that if we are to understand each other we need to ask the question: why do you see the world and other people like this? There is of course no simple answer to this, but ignoring a field of research which suggests some of the reasons for our behaviour and our feelings and emotions denies us the possibility of understanding.

Phoebe's interest and passion and her need to share her knowledge provide us with a vital perspective. The information provided in the book is essential, but perhaps as important is the sharing of those characteristics. When we seek to understand each other we need to bring to the journey those imperatives: the desire to understand and to have the courage to take a journey into worlds we do not know.

Chapter 1: Introduction

A week ago, I was driving home across the moors on a thick, gloomy day. As I came round the corner, a shaft of sunlight elbowed aside the clouds and lit up one field, diamond sharp, so brilliant that my whole attention was claimed by it. It felt as if I could count each tussock, every blade of grass and the droplets of water shining on each one. It was a moment of total clarity snatched from the murk.

If one has written as many books as I have on a single subject, there has to be an extremely good reason for embarking on another; something especially fascinating which throws new light on one's focus of interest. This book is a detective enquiry. I am trying to construct a story that marries the avalanche of neurobiological research pouring out from a wide range of professional journals, with approaches being used in care, and at the same time listening to the voices of people with autism. For comparison, since I hope that it will bring more understanding to those of us not on the autistic spectrum, it contains material that is personal – and I am the person I know best.

Currently, in the rush for empirical evidence, burgeoning understanding of underlying processes is not always getting transferred from theory into practice – and on the other hand, researchers are not always pursuing new directions highlighted by the extensive experience of front-line workers. Neither are we listening to what people with autism are telling us.

Part of the problem is that autism research covers such a wide field. Each branch is publishing in its own particular journals, therefore references to the relevant literature are not necessarily picked up by those who are working at the face of autism. For example, research on pain caused by trigeminal neuralgia, and sometimes overlooked in autism, is mainly to be found in dental journals, since dentists are the first port of call for those with pain in the jaw. Trigeminal neuralgia is characterised by the adult or child chewing and applying pressure with their fingers to relieve acute pain just under and behind the ear lobes.[1]

'In the midst of a meteoric rise in the rates of autism significant new research into physical symptoms has been done. The challenge is to incorporate this new research into the practice of medicine that historically has stereotyped autism as a purely psychiatric disorder.'[2]

---

1   For more information about trigeminal neuralgia see Chapter 2 in Caldwell P (2014) *The Anger Box*. Brighton: Pavilion Publishing & Media Ltd.

2   Kerm JK, Geier D, Sykes L & Geier R (2015) Relevance of neuroinflammation and encephalitis in autism. *Frontiers in Cellular Neuroscience* **9** (128) 519.

As the title suggests, *Hall of Mirrors – Shards of Clarity* refers to two states. It is an exploration triggered by a number of themes which have surfaced and converged during recent work and reading, so it covers a wide canvas. Inevitably it is an idiosyncratic and personal selection – but I hope its somewhat zig-zag hunt for clues may be of interest and assistance to those of us who are involved in shaping care pathways. As before, it builds on the work of others in order to reach some sort of synthesis.

In trying to understand the processes that underlie autism, we have reached a stage that moves beyond behavioural observation to complex neuroscience and neuroanatomy. I have tried to limit the more technical descriptions; where this is not possible I have simplified the language as much as possible. As an author, I am struggling with the interconnectivity of subjects that branch off in multiple directions. It is not easy to find one's way through the thicket of information; there are too many fascinating trails. Some are hard for the non-specialist to understand and some turn out to be dead ends. To start simple I am going to begin with a snapshot from my own childhood.

As a small girl I am taken on a trip to Madame Tussauds, galleries full of waxworks, each immobile on their platforms, groups of the famous and infamous, heroes, celebrities and villains immortalised in wax – but still, in human terms, undemanding and non-threatening as tailor's dummies. All goes well until we move into the 'Hall of Mirrors'.

Suddenly, everything I know as real explodes, my own image, all that I perceived as myself swims and slithers, as if I am being pulled in all directions. What I know of as my self, my physical image, disintegrates: I burst into tears and have to be taken outside to be comforted.

So if a loss of sense of self can have this rather overdramatic effect on a securely attached child, what is it that is so vital about our personal image – and why does a threat to it leave us so intimidated? In this respect, what is the feeling of the aloneness of autism, where does it come from? What is it that leaves those on the spectrum so particularly vulnerable? Are there ways we can make it easier for individuals with autism to be their selves and relate to people other than themselves?

Emerging from my identity crisis, triggered by the Hall of Mirrors, 'shards of clarity', is a phrase used by six-year-old Arran's mother, following a visit to her family to demonstrate how one might use a child's body language to develop emotional engagement (Intensive Interaction). While Arran does not have a diagnosis of autism, there are a number of features of his behaviour (such as attachment to repetitive behaviour and an apparent difficulty in engaging in personal relationships), that remind one of life on the spectrum.

Arran has a rare genetic mutation. He is registered as having a severe sight impairment, although he does register movement and will stand nose-to-nose with the TV or watch flickering fingers, attempting to draw them closer to his face. After observing an intervention I did with Arran using his sounds and rhythms to communicate with him (Intensive Interaction), his mother said that whereas before, although she had witnessed the effect of using body language to tune into a child, she had not 'got it' but now she saw its potential. She told me later that after I had left she had spent hours sitting on her bed playing with him. For the first time, she and her son had been able to relate to each other. She added that, for Arran, it was as if 'shards of clarity' had come into his world, a world that until now had been making no sense to him.

This is a striking image: fragments of coherence in an environment that presents the brain with sensory chaos, one where swirling pixillated images combine with capricious sounds and overwhelming bodily sensations.

The sensory experience of each autistic child or adult is different; this is how Iris Johansson describes how it felt for her:

'It made my body feel like an unmoving piece of meat that often hurt. Then there were dangerous demons and horrible noises that scared the wits out of me. Then I would often scream, bang my head and scream until it quieted. The light was so unpleasant in the ordinary world. Everything changed constantly and my head burned and ached.'[3].

No wonder a child or adult with autism recoils from a world that physically threatens to overwhelm them and grasps at any stimulus he or she does recognise like iron filings to a magnet.

If we imagine taking the top off our heads and looking inside, we shall see the familiar two halves of the brain. Somewhat like a walnut, they are joined across the middle by a band of fibres called the corpus callosum. Another of the starting points for this particular book arose out of being asked to help find ways to assist a young woman with autism, who also has a diagnosis of damage to this bridge between the two halves of her brain. Trying to unravel what this might mean in terms of behaviour, my attention was drawn to two rather different sources. The first was an astonishing book (and accompanying film) by Jill Bolte Taylor[4]. Jill

---

3   Johansson I (2012) *A Different Childhood*. Arizona: Inkwell Productions.

4   Bolte Taylor J (2008) *My Stroke of Insight*. London: Hodder & Stoughton.

is a neuro-anatomist. Her research involves post-mortem studies of the brain in relation to mental illness and particularly schizophrenia. At the age of 37, she suffered a severe stroke. Half her brain was flooded with blood – and she literally observed the progress of her stroke with a scientist's eye while her left hemisphere shut down. She had access to both the 'inside-out point of view' of the trauma she was experiencing, as well as a scientist's observations from the 'outside-in'. She was able to follow the process of failure in the left brain.

Jill's contingent outside-in and inside-out experience into left hand/right hand brain functioning is complimented by the research of Michael Gazziniga, a cognitive neuroscientist. Michael and his team and have spent forty years investigating the neural functioning of patients with severe epilepsy who have undergone surgical treatment to sever the corpus callosum, effectively cutting off the two halves of the brain from each other.

Another starting point has been the number of accounts by people on the autistic spectrum who report their experience of blurred boundaries and the loss of a sense of self[5]. In order to describe their different states of sensory experience they use words such as 'in' or 'out'. There are semantic complications to this: while Donna Williams contrasts the chaos she experiences in the outer world with her inner retreat, Iris Johansson uses 'inside' and 'outside' in the opposite sense throughout her book . For Iris, 'out' is when she is lost in her own world (one might think of this in terms of being 'spaced out'). But for Donna, 'out' refers to the world outside her personal inside hideout.

Overall this book is asking what happens to one's sense of self if one's brain is receiving a distorted image of the world and its intentions towards oneself, so that much of one's intake is experienced as hostile, triggering the body's self-defence system.

'Not having a clear sense of my boundaries, what is me and what is not me? My personal space feels threatened and invaded.'[6]

In addition to defensive strategies, such as repetitive behaviours, avoidance, shut down or aggression to self or others to avoid the perceived source of one's distress, some people on the spectrum will adopt what appear to be different personalities (manifest by different voices) to shield their vulnerability, even a number of these. However, they appear to be bewildered rather than schizophrenic. So what is happening to them? Why do they feel so disembodied?

---

5   Caldwell P (2014) *The Anger Box*. Brighton: Pavilion Publishers and Media Ltd.

6   Personal communication with an autistic person.

'Consciousness' and 'sense of self' are difficult subjects and I do not intend to become embroiled in complex philosophical arguments – but rather to approach them from the point of view of a practitioner, by way of asking what it is that people who have lost any such certainty are telling us about their experience and what does this tell us about our own experience of who we feel we are? Is there anything we can do to support those who are trapped by such a loss?

Finally, I have become increasingly aware of the crucial importance of a subject that I have already written about and that is, autistic or not, the primacy of our need for **confirmation**. What do we understand by confirmation? Why do we need it and what does it do for us? How does it relate to proprioception[7] and anxiety? And to go back to the title, where does confirmation fit into the image of shards of clarity, as used by Arran's other?

---

7   Proprioception is the sensory feedback from our muscles and joints which tells the brain what the body is doing and where it is in space. We shall be looking at this in detail in Chapter 9.

Chapter 2: Body language

Do I have to be able to use words in order to tell you how I feel? Can I let you know I am miserable if we can't use words?

I think that all of us would agree that we usually know if a person is dejected or happy simply by their body language, their posture and their facial expression. And we adjust our approach and responses accordingly.

For those of us who use body language to communicate with people who find it difficult to tell us what they feel and need – and with whom we find it difficult to engage – we have long been aware that emotion is expressed by **how** people make their verbal or non-verbal utterances, rather than the specific sounds they make, words they say, or the actions they perform. It is the way they perform communications that allows us to gauge their affective state, how they are feeling, particularly whether they are relaxed or stressed. When we are using the language their brain is familiar with, the connection is mutual. A father said of his six-year-old son, 'This is the first time I have felt myself in his mind'.

And when we think of using body language to tune into people with autism, a point that is sometimes overlooked is that while our conversation partner may or may not find it difficult to decode our body language, we can read theirs. This is what tells us how they are feeling. We need to watch, watch, watch with all our senses, tuning into their state of mind.

In terms of understanding how people feel, we pick this up from the way they make sounds, their intonations and rhythms. Having learned to speak, we still continue accompanying our spoken language with the non-verbal language of gesture and posture – the two run side-by-side. We may refer to a person as 'wooden' if their body language gives us no clue as to how they feel.

Based on the strength of their brain responses, one of the McGill University's research group's most intriguing findings is that we tend to pick out how people are saying things rather than what they are saying to us[8]. Focusing on three emotions, happiness, anger and sadness, the authors demonstrated that people's

---

8   Pell MD, Rothermich K, Liu P, Paulmann S, Sethi S & Rigoulot S (2015) Preferential decoding of emotion from human non-linguistic vocalisations versus speech prosody. *Biological Psychology* **111** 14–25

attention is attracted more quickly when emotions are conveyed through non-verbal sounds rather than when the same emotions are relayed through speech. This is particularly true when the emotion expressed is anger.

'The identification of emotional vocalisations depends on systems in our brains that pre-date the development of speech in evolutionary terms. Understanding emotions in spoken language on the other hand, involves more recent brain systems that have evolved as human language developed...Vocalisations which are relatively unconstrained by the segmental structure of language (sounds, not speech) emanate in large part from glottal and sub-glottal activities associated with autonomic/physiological response to emotion'. [9]

In other words, spoken language is symbolic and involves immensely complex motor co-ordination systems which take place close to the jaw. The listener's brain has to interpret the content of what they are saying. On the other hand, non-verbal sounds (together with gestures and posture) fast-track our attention onto how people *feel*, a facility that was necessary and in evolutionary terms one which developed long before language. With respect to autism, people who are anxious (as people on the spectrum are), are particularly sensitive to emotional voices[10].

They are what one might call, 'socially hypersensitive'. In a non-autistic context, a colleague described them as developing 'emotional vigilance'. So it is not only the sense of the communication that is a problem; it can be the affect that is conveyed. A friend on the spectrum describes the response of her nervous system to any form of emotional warmth as like being 'hit by an emotional taser'.

This is a particularly powerful metaphor and we need to pause for a minute and take on board what this might mean in terms of bodily sensations worked out in our own body. Bear in mind that for some individuals on the spectrum, the hair trigger can be set off by such ordinary events as using a person's name, or by addressing them in direct speech. Simply by refraining from their use, we can avoid plunging them into sensory overload.

While there is a statistic that two-thirds of what we take from interactions with other people are derived from their body language (rather than from the information they present to us), this is widely quoted out of context[11]. Nevertheless, the biological imperative during any interaction is always lurking somewhere in our minds, 'Do I trust this person enough to bother with what they are telling me (or should I run? Do they want to attack, eat, or mate?)' – and

9   Trouvain J (2014) Laughing, breathing and clicking – the prosody of non-verbal vocalisations. *Speech Prosody* 598-602.

10   Caldwell P (2014) *The Anger Box*. Brighton: Pavilion Publishers and Media Ltd.

11   Mehrabian A & Ferris SR (1967) Inference of attitudes from nonverbal communication in two channels. *Journal of Consulting Psychology* **31** (3) 248–252.

perhaps one should add, 'Do they want to manipulate my response for their own end?' Our understanding of this derives from our conversation partner's posture, gestures, tone of voice and facial language. We know fairly accurately where we are on the scale of being hugged or mugged.

It's not just people: we can trace this ability to map each other's feelings non-verbally back to our non-human ancestors. If we turn our attention to primates, while there is still a debate as to whether or not they have the capacity to 'learn' human symbolic communication, what is very clear is that in the wild, they do interact with each other using body language. For example, mountain gorillas live in groups and they use sounds to keep in touch when travelling – but also to demonstrate their feelings. Within the group, mutual grooming reduces potential aggression and who grooms who (intimate body language), maintains the pecking order.

When challenged by another male, a classic example is the use of intimidatory body language in the ritual aggressive behaviour of silverback gorillas. In order to avoid actually having to fight, which may be lethal, they stand erect (making themselves look larger), increase their hooting sounds, beat their chests, pull up vegetation and throw it at their rivals, beat the ground with cupped fists and emit strong odour. There is no question that the alpha male is ordering the younger male to back off.

Recently I was asked by his mother to visit Kavee, a small boy with a diagnosis of autism spectrum disorder (ASD) and attention deficit hyperactivity disorder (ADHD). Kavee is 10 years old. He has no speech and is very restless. This is our first meeting. When I arrive at his house, his mother calls upstairs to him and asks him to come downstairs and say, 'Hello' to me. (This is a commonly made mistake. As we shall see when we meet another child, Pranve, in order to avoid raising the level of a child or adult's sensory overload, it is important to try and introduce oneself in their personal language before invading their personal space.)

Kavee walks towards me with his hand stretched out politely (this is what he has been taught to do), takes mine – and digs his thumbnail hard into the back of my hand. It hurts and the message is clear: 'Back off'. So my first question is, what should I make of this behaviour? And while respecting his desire to be left alone, is there anything that can be done to help him feel less threatened? I gently but firmly squeeze his hand back to acknowledge his message.

At this time of the morning, Kavee would normally have expected to be going out for a walk. So while I talk to his mother in the adjacent sitting room, he patrols up and down by the front door making anxious noises. Based on the premise that we all express to each other how we feel through our body language, I answer these with empathetic sounds, not by imitating them exactly, but rather by listening and responding to the affective quality of each sound. After a few minutes he becomes less restless and joins us. In terms of prosody, pitch, rhythm, taking turns and 'call and response', I am able to engage him in a non-verbal conversation about the anxiety that is currently dominating his life. I am tuning into this anxiety.

By way of reducing his anxiety, Kavee swipes his iPad, flicking through it endlessly, not to obtain a particular program but rather (in a world that is sensorily overloading his brain) using it as an effect he can control: he flicks, something moves. Like Temple Grandin[12], who tells us that as a child she endlessly spun a coin and used her profound attention to this activity to cut out all other incoming sensory stimuli, Kavee focuses on this flicker, so he does not have to listen and attend to what is going on around him.

Kavee also plays with his fingers, flexing and extending them in such a way that suggests he is giving himself proprioceptive stimuli[13]. He not only feels sensations, but he takes this feeling on board, so he knows what he is doing. It gives him access to some level of coherence. I show his mother how to engage with him through these movements and he responds by moving to sit close to her and enjoying this interaction. Now she is responding to him with signals that have significance for him, aligning herself with how he feels by the manner in which she responds. They are using his language to talk about how he is feeling, and interacting in a pleasurable way that has immediate meaning for his brain without overloading his speech processing system.

Kavee likes powerful proprioceptive signals that have meaning for him. His mother says he particularly enjoys bouncing on a trampoline. Catching his attention, I use a gesture to point to the trampoline in Kavee's garden and flex my knees up and down. He gets my message at once, grins and we go out into the garden. He climbs on the trampoline and I stand outside the netting, bobbing up and down. Joining in the rhythm of his jumps, I use his sounds to reinforce the rhythm of our interaction. He bounces over to me and, standing inside the netting, presses his hands and face on mine. We rock backwards and forwards. He is smiling. Instead of his initial rejection, with the boundary of the netting between us we have found a safe way of enjoying each other's company and being with each other. There is now no need for him to feel threatened. His spontaneous outreach to me is very moving.

---

12 Grandin T (1992) *A is for Autism* film. Available on YouTube.

13 Proprioception refers to messages from the muscles and joints to the brain, telling it what it is doing. So if we stand on our toes, we feel pressure in our toes, calves and thighs, telling us we are standing on tip-toe. Similarly, if we are sitting down, we feel pressure on our feet and backside, telling us of our seated position.

Next he does the same with his mother. Then he goes to the other side of the trampoline. When she follows him he repeats his engagement with her. Afterwards, when he comes in, he is very relaxed. He takes off his outdoor shoes, puts them in the cupboard and shuts the door without being asked, something his mother has been trying to persuade him to do, unsuccessfully, up until now.

In the chapter on proprioception (Chapter 9) we will return to the reduction in tension consequent to introducing rhythmic jolts. For now, the trampoline jolts have put meaningful signals into his brain, his anxiety is reduced and he is able to focus his brain on the task of placing his shoes in the cupboard, which he already knows about, but until now has been unable to organise. This is similar to the effect of jolts produced by using a pogo stick described by Judith Bluestone, a neurologist who has autism, in *The Fabric of Autism*. These and other examples suggest that introduction of rhythmic stimuli reduces anxiety (since it introduces stimuli in a form that have meaning for the brain, and allows it to focus on completion of motor activities that have previously been blocked)[14].

Later on I shall be looking in more detail at what can be learned from this intervention with Kavee. But for the time being, I want to draw your attention to our need to listen to qualitative engagement as well as to summarising quantitative conclusions from empirical research. If we do not attend to the affective quality of what the body language of those who are living an experience is conveying to us, how they are feeling, either through speech or body language, we may be focusing our investigations towards answering ancillary or misleading questions.

Typically in autism, what the non-autistic world sees as behavioural problems relate to anxiety, trauma and pain. We should be focusing our attention on these root causes rather than better ways of containment.

Hall of Mirrors – Shards of Clarity is about the inner world of autism, about distortion, warped signals, and the desperate search for coherence in a world full of floating fragments, noisy static and imbalance, where the continuous question that needs to be answered is, 'Is what I am experiencing real, or is it not real?'[15].

Living in a world where everything is potentially hostile and the only solution on offer is retreat into an inner world, Donna Williams tells us: 'All the relationships one should have had with the world outside one are with oneself'.[16]

---

14   Bluestone J (2005) *The Fabric of Autism*. Sapphire Enterprises.

15   Caldwell P (2014) *The Anger Box*. Chapter 9. Brighton: Pavilion Publishers and Media Ltd.

16   Williams D (1996) *Jam-Jar*. Channel 4 programme. Glasgow: Fresh Film and Television.

Part of the message of this book is that behaviours which are seen as socially unacceptable are a consequence of neurological dysfunction, arising ultimately from genetic fragility or environmental pressure, which, during development, hinder the fulfilment of what might be called a master plan. The figures are startling. For example, research suggests that 69% of children with ASD diagnosis also have microglial activation or neuro-inflammation of the brain which may be treatable[17,18].

Regions of the brain fail to connect because nerves grow in the wrong directions, or fail to grow, or overgrow. The wiring is haywire. Thresholds for switching organs on or off get set at the wrong levels. Like the child in the hall of mirrors, what Kavee and those like him are struggling with is that his environment (and therefore he himself and how he might relate to it) does not make sense to him. On top of this, what are seen as socially different or deviant responses are frequently misunderstood and targeted by both peers and ill-informed adults so that, rather than receiving support, they report being bullied.

Even taking into account the gap between research and practice, we can find ways of reaching into their world and making it more intelligible, by offering a combined approach that includes:

- addressing their sensory difficulties

- using communication based on feedback that is in turn based on an individual's own body language, offering tailored signals that are easily processed and act as markers that have meaning in what is perceived as a hostile environment

- offering powerful kinaesthetic (physical) signals to help confirm physical sense of self

- offering positive support to confirm the psychological sense of self.

---

17 Microglial cells are small glial cells found in the central nervous system which basically act as cleaners, mopping up plaques, damaged or unnecessary neurons and synapses, and infectious agents. They do not conduct electrical impulses.

18 Kern JK, Geier DA, Sykes L & Geier M R (2015) Relevance of neuroinflammation and encephalitis in autism. *Frontiers in Cellular Neuroscience* **9** 519.

Chapter 3: Grey world

This chapter is about the information that our senses receive and send to the brain and what the brain does with the information, what picture it builds for us of the world we live in and its intentions towards us. Do you see what I see, hear what I hear? Do we all get the same picture?

I shall start with the perceptions of the non-autistic world. Discussing his research on sensory perception, David Eagleman[19] points out that (autistic or not), we are severely limited in our ability to pick up on what the world round us is doing. For example, our brains simply do not possess the necessary organs to take on board the echo location possessed by bats, or the magnetic homing of migratory birds. Our bodies are transparent, not only to email conversations in transit but also to a whole range of waves from infra-red to x-rays and neutrinos: we have no access to these modes of information-harvesting, since we do not possess the necessary sensors to detect them.

Visible light, the stuff we see, is less than one ten millionth of the electromagnetic spectrum[20]. The rest is made up of everything from short wavelength gamma rays to long wavelength radio waves: because we have no receptors that recognise Wi-Fi and microwaves, we are unable to eavesdrop on the cell-phone messages sneaking through our bodies unread.

But there is more out there: dark matter, the eighty-five per cent of unmeasurable cosmic substance, whose existence is only inferred from the effect that it has on gravity. We really don't know much about what is going on around us!

Eagleman points to the useful idea encapsulated in the German word, 'umwelt' to describe the world we perceive (as opposed to the actual reality out there). We fail to recognise the umwelt of others, assuming that our own umwelt is all there is.

However, not only do we need functioning receptive organs but also, when these have registered an incoming signal, the neural pathway between the receptor and the interpreting brain has to be wired up properly. And by 'properly', I mean using the pathway that is most effective in delivering the message to its correct processing destination, so that hearing messages end up at hearing processing targets and not at visual processing targets (as can happen in synaesthesia, where there is a cross over between sensory pathways on the way to their destinations).

---

19   Eagleman D (2015) Can We Create New Senses for Humans? TED Talk. Available at: www.ted. com/talks/david_eagleman_can_we_create_new_senses_for_humans (accessed September 2017).

20   Eagleman D (2015) *The Brain: The story of you*. London: Canongate Books.

Autistic people may spend their entire lives dedicated to the search for coherence, looking for something that has meaning. In a world that is providing a chaotic picture, the brain spends its whole time trying to pick up recognisable patterns, something that makes sense; anything which it can cling on to. For our part we can be so misled when we stray unwittingly into somebody else's umwelt, particularly the autistic world. It is not only autistic people who are poor at seeing the world from other people's point of view; we are all poor at Theory of Mind[21].

Sensory distortions mean that children and adults on the autistic spectrum are living in a totally different sensory landscape. Or perhaps it would be more accurate to say that their interpretations of the same landscape are very different from those of us who are not on the spectrum. It is extremely difficult for us to suspend our own sensory experience and take on board what it is like to live in this different landscape. It is not just enough to know, for example, that objects may have no boundaries so you can't tell where they are, and they may be moving around and seen as threatening and invasive: what does this feel like? Letting go of our own agendas and emptying it of all that is familiar to us requires positive effort on our behalf.

Before returning to autism, I want to look at the extraordinary plasticity of the brain, and how it can learn to compensate for injury or deficit by re-routing signals from one processing area to another.

For me, and I assume for you, we are constantly on the lookout, assessing what is going on, trying to build up a topographical image of our surroundings since our brains need to protect us in order to survive. We use our eyes and ears and our sensations of touch, taste and smell to advise ourselves of the situation we are in. But suppose we are one of the one in ten adults in Britain who are colour blind, a condition that involves confusion of colours, the most common being red with green. We shall have to learn that the top traffic light signals danger and also we shall have to compensate for our lack of colour awareness.

Moreover, one in 33,000 people have monochromatic vision. They see the world in shades of grey, as if it were a black and white TV. Surprisingly, their sensory experience of their surroundings may be closer to the real world out there than that of those of the rest of us (trichromats) who experience it in colour, since colour is an optical illusion. Today I look out of my window at a range of limestone hills; fresh with new grass, bright with spring green, splashes of gold where the early morning sun strikes their folds. And yet, contrary to what I believe because my perceptions tell me so, it's dull out there. Visual signals reach my eyes in the

---

21   Baron Cohen S, Leslie A M & Frith U (1985) Does the autistic child have a theory of mind? *Cognition* **21** 37–46.

form of electromagnetic signals and my eyes translate these into electro-chemical messages which are transmitted to my brain, which interprets the different wave lengths as different colours[22]. The verdant dales have no colour.

However, it's not only seeing colour and even form that is an illusion. Just as strange is the idea that there is no sound out there. All the sounds I hear; my fingers tapping on the keyboard, a car passing outside, a man calling his dog in the car park, a song thrush imitating the warning signal of an ambulance in reverse, are no more than pressure waves entering my ear, converting to electro-chemical signals that are sent to my brain and turned into sounds. I live on a tectonic fault line. Were the earth's plates to collide or slide over each other, as they have done in the past, the immediate affect would be that minute hairs in my ear would pick up the pressure waves and transmit these to my brain. Only then would I hear noise and get the message; 'Run'.

But it comes as even more of a shock (literally an eye-opener) to hear that we do not actually need to be able to have functional eyes in order to be able to see. Born with cancer, Daniel Kish has had both his eyes removed by the time he was thirteen months old. He now walks round the world confidently using a long stick but more unusually, he makes clicks with his tongue which act as a sonar system.

'My clicks (or sometimes hisses), resemble flashes of sound that go out and reach the surfaces around me and return to me with patterns which are pieces of information much as light does for you, like the sonar system of a bat.' [23]

Although Daniel is blind he uses sound to see. His 'sound flashes' are transmitted to Daniel's brain, where his visual cortex has learned to interpret and form images from them. He demonstrates the principle by asking the audience to close their eyes and hiss to a panel in front of his face. He then moves the panel to and fro: the echo sounds different, reflecting its relative position. (It is quite easy to test this. Hold an A4 size book in front of your mouth and move it backwards and forwards while making a hissing sound and hear the difference). As a result of extreme focus Daniel's capacity to listen (rather than using his hearing, which is within the normal range), has become extremely acute. Asked to describe his picture of the world, he says his sonar works behind him as well as in front, a kind of fuzzy, three-dimensional, surface geometry. He tells us that one of his students described his own hearing as so acute that he can hear and see through walls; he describes it as something like having X-ray vision.

---

22   Eagleman D (2015) *The Brain: The story of you*. Edinburgh: Canongate.

23   Kish D (2015) *How I Use Sonar to Navigate the World*. Ted Talk. Available at: https://www.ted.com/talks/daniel_kish_how_i_use_sonar_to_navigate_the_world (accessed September 2017).

Just how plastic is the brain in terms of sensory processing? When Daniel describes his perception of the world around him as 'seeing', does he build up a picture of his surroundings through sound echolocation (one which would use the auditory cortex to process incoming signals)? Or is his brain relocating the sound signals to the visual cortex? Remarkably, scans show that it is the visual cortex of the brain that is processing the signals rather than the auditory cortex[24].

Daniel has taught his skill to many people with no sight. A young man, Ben Underwood, also developed clicking independently in order to navigate[25]. Ben demonstrates his skill on roller skates rounding between obstacles such as two closely parked cars without touching them. More difficult, because its curved surfaces scatter the signals, he can locate a thin rod standing up on a table. He can also pick out two identical small objects from a number of others placed in front of him; all this just by clicking his tongue.

It is not only sonar echo signals that can be interpreted as vision by the visual cortex. Paul Bach-y-Rita, professor at the University of Wisconsin, believes our sensory perception is interchangeable to an unimaginable degree and has demonstrated that the brain can use the visual cortex to interpret signals picked up by the tongue. A video camera strapped to the forehead of a blindfolded man is used to feed in visual signals (converted to pixels) through a plastic strip inserted in the mouth) to a grid of electrodes placed on the tongue. The subject is then asked to 'catch' a ball that is rolled to him on the left or right hand sides. Although he can neither hear nor see the ball, a tingling passes over his tongue acting as a map, telling him which side to reach out to so that he is able to capture the ball[26].

'In normal vision, the eyes send signals to the middle of the brain. It forwards these to the visual cortex at the back of the brain. When sensing with the tongue, the brain learns to interpret touch signals in the visual cortex.'[27]

Based on these principles, Professor Bach-y-Rita has developed a helmet, 'Brainport', which is being used to help non-sighted people navigate the world around them[28].

---

24 Haler L, Arnott S & Goodale M (2011) Neural correlates of natural human echolocation in early and late blind echolocation experts. *PLOS One* **6** (5).

25 *The Boy Who Sees Without Eyes* (2007) Extraordinary People documentary series, currently available on YouTube.

26 Abrams M & Winters D (2013) *Can You See With Your Tongue?* [online] Discover Magazine. Available at: http://discovermagazine.com/2003/jun/feattongue (accessed September 2017).

27 Quote from *'Blind Learn to See with Tongue'*, segment on CBS news. Available at: https://www.youtube.com/watch?v=OKd56D2mvN0. (accessed September 2017).

28 Kendrick M (2009) *Tasting the Light: Device lets the blind "see" with their tongues*. Scientific American. Available at: www.scientificamerican.com/article/device-lets-blind-see-with-tongues/ (accessed September 2017).

We need to re-think 'seeing', as not just taking in information with our eyes and knowing what our environment looks like. Seeing is in the brain, which wants to see, and does not much care about what the inputs are and where they come from. In the case of vision, it may be a question of activating the visual cortex to process non-visual information. The incoming information (of clicks through the ears or the signals from the tongue), eventually feeds through to the visual cortex (re-routing?), which it learns to process and interpret as seeing[29].

It is not only senses that come in through visible organs such as the eye, ear, nose and tongue that are potentially interchangeable, but also touch and pressure. Take for example the reading of braille through our kinesthetic sense, using finger tips, where the blind 'see' the letters and words. Using brain scans, Pascual-Leone showed that it is the visual cortex that lights up. When sighted people performed the same task there was no activity in the visual cortex[30].

While it is not clear exactly how information which comes through the sense of touch ends up being processed in the visual cortex so that the person gets a visual picture rather than a tactile map, Pascual-Leone suggests that the glial cells[31] may be involved. One of their functions is aiding in (or preventing, in some instances) recovery from neural injury.[32]

It is not only visual deficits that can be compensated for. David Eagleman has designed a vest to be worn by deaf people which uses mobile phone technology to convert patterns of incoming sound frequencies into vibrations which are felt by the wearer, converted into electro-chemical signals which are transmitted to the brain, which the brain then translates back into words. With only a little practice the deaf wearer can hear and repeat the words which he has not heard directly through his ears[33]. In this case, sound, which the vest user is unable to hear, is converted to pressure signals which are fed to the brain and converted back into sound.

So far, in order to illustrate the astonishing plasticity of the brain, we have been addressing sensory processing deficits which have arisen from developmental failures or injury, and looking at how the brain can learn to re-route its pathway and find a way round the deficit. Let's turn now to another form of cross-wiring

29 Abrams M & Winters D (2013) Can You See With Your Tongue? Discover Magazine. Available at: http://discovermagazine.com/2003/jun/feattongue (accessed September 2017).

30 Sadato N, Pascual-Leone A, Grafman J, Ibañez V, Deiber MP, Dold G & Hallett M (1996) Activation of the primary visual cortex by braille reading in blind subjects. *Nature* **380** 6574 526–528.

31 Glial cells are non-neuronal cells which outnumber neurons in the brain by three to one and among other functions are involved in synaptic pruning, cutting back unused nerve cells.

32 Purves D, Augustine GJ, Fitzpatrick D, Katz LC, LaMantia A-S, McNamara JO & Williams SM (2001) *Neuroscience* (2nd edition). Sunderland, MA: Sinauer Associates.

33 Eagleman D (2015) *The Brain: The story of you* (p168). Edinburgh: Canongate.

known as synesthesia: one in two hundred of the general population experiences synesthesia, where one sense is always cross-wired with another. In his book on synesthesia, Cytowic quotes a synesthete:

'When I listen to music I see shapes on an externalised area about twelve inches in front of my face... sounds are most easily likened to oscilloscope configurations – lines moving in colour, often metallic in colour, with height, width and depth. My favourite music has lines that extend horizontally beyond the screen area.' [34]

Synesthesia is even more common among the autistic world. Iris Johansson gives us an extraordinarily vivid description of the effects of synesthesia on her auditory intake during her autistic childhood:

'I loved to bite small children. They screamed bloody murder and this sound pleased me and I could not understand why I was not allowed to bite them. The atmosphere got so beautiful from the child's screaming and even more from the upset feelings that the grownups around contributed in addition.' [35]

The reason for this apparently perverted pleasure emerges later in the book, where she describes how her brain was interpreting the sounds, and what she was getting out of it. Iris really enjoyed being scolded: when this happened her mother's words flew around and formed shapes:

'It was different lights that sparkled. It was beautiful and you could never predict how it would look. I stood there and was entranced. I flowed into colours, shapes, patterns and let myself be carried back and forth up and down. Everything changed shape continuously and I flowed with it.' [36]

Iris and her mother were extracting totally different sensory interpretations from the same situation. While Iris saw beautiful ribbons of light that calmed her, her mother was wrestling with a completely 'impossible' child. And she had absolutely no idea of what was motivating Iris' extraordinary behaviour.

Synesthesia is just one of the mis-wirings that can so mislead us when we stray unwittingly into somebody else's umwelt – but at least once we know about it, Iris' behavior begins to make sense. When she heard a bellowing baby, she did literally see the ribbons and colored lights. One gets the impression from her descriptions (of the visual sensations that sound triggers in her brain when she hears a baby screaming), as like being surrounded by an aurora borealis of great

---

34   Cytowic RE (2002) *Synesthesia: A union of the senses* (2nd edition). Cambridge, MA: The MIT Press.
35   Johansson I (1995) *A Different Childhood*. Scottsdale, AZ: Inkwell Productions.
36   *Ibid.*

beauty that sparkled, one that was enhanced by the angry double bass responses of adult remonstration. From the social point of view, Iris' additional problem is that her brain has learned to link a positive sensory experience with a negative behavior.

Synesthesia is three times as common in individuals with autism as in the non-autistic population. Ramachandran suggests that synesthesia is inherited since it runs in families, arising during development, when a gene that should have a local expression, expresses itself more widely, so there are lots of excess connections. Such hyper-connectivity facilitates the linking of two unrelated processing systems, especially those that are near neighbours in the brain.[37] According to Cytowic,[38] the commonest from of synesthesia is seeing letters or words as colours but any combination of sensory swap-overs is possible. He describes a colleague who told him his over-salted soup had too many triangles in it. Jenny, a woman with whom I was working, would throw her plate of food on the floor shouting, 'I can't eat that, it's too black!'. She was experiencing taste as colours.

As a colleague remarked to me as we discussed Iris, since we base our assumptions and strategies on our own sensory experience, 'where on earth would one start in terms of practice?'

---

37   Ramachandran VS (2007) *3 Clues to Understanding Your Brain*. TEDTalk. Available at: https://www.ted.com/talks/vilayanur_ramachandran_on_your_mind (accessed September 2017).

38   Cytowic RE (2003) *The Man Who Tasted Shapes*. Cambridge, MA: MIT Press.

Chapter 4: Connections

Sensory processing seems so simple to those of us who have a fully functional system of sense perception and response. We receive a sensory input, process it and respond in one smooth ongoing process which we do not have to think about consciously. It just happens. But in practice there are many layers involved. Assuming our sense organs are in working order and correctly converting the incoming stimulus, there is the problem of filtering it from 'unimportant background inputs', followed by recognition and directing it to the correct processing destination without it getting lost on the way or scrambled with other inputs, not to speak of comparison with related information and finally, being able to respond.

If I want to tell you something, I may know what I want to say but find it impossible to sequence the words and coordinate the motor movements necessary to articulate the words. At a low level, I may recognise rhythms that underpin sentences rather than the words themselves. A friend with dementia is in the last days of her life. Although we are close, she does not recognise me but lies in bed scratching the sheet. I answer the rhythm of her scratches. She immediately takes notice, tilts her head towards the sound and listens for more.

Eagleman's vest (mentioned in the previous chapter) offers hope not only to those who are deaf. It may also bring communication and relief from anxiety, even if at a very simple level, to those whose severe disability limits them to pattern recognition. Their need is great.

When messages do reach the interpreting areas of the brain (but before we can respond), they have to run the gauntlet of a risk assessment system which judges whether they are hostile, user-friendly, or are meaningless and can be ignored. Finally, we all have different thresholds for triggering alarm signals and, if the signal is judged to be dangerous, setting off the body's self-defence system. Due to over-sensitive reception systems in the autistic brain, the threshold for triggering negative responses may be set very low indeed. An input that appears benign for the non-autistic person may be terrifying for those on the spectrum. A particular voice at a normal level may be experienced as excruciatingly painful.

But still, we all presume that our own umwelt is shared by everyone else, and because of the hyper- and hypo-sensitivities and consequent distortions experienced by autistic people, much of their sensory experience registers as threatening, and consequently anxiety-provoking, to the point where Therese Jolliffe speaks of living in terror all the time[39].

In the search for more understanding, investigations into autism are turning attention away from behaviour (what we outsiders see), towards neurobiological structure (what is experienced by the person from the inside). The picture that is emerging is of extensive neurological damage, in the sense that systems are not being wired up in such a way as to be optimally effective. This is complicated by the fact that the actual pattern of distortions differs in different individuals. While the brain of some people on the spectrum will show damage in one area, this may be intact in another. From the point of view of the outsider trying to understand what autism means at a cellular level and the emerging picture of neurobiological chaos, it is extraordinary that people on the spectrum can extract any sense at all out of the world we share. However the way that autism is viewed has changed radically. Neuro-imaging studies by Courchesne directed attention to autism as being a neurological disorder rather than a psychological one[40]. There may be overgrowth or undergrowth of neurones and neuronal pathways, and many different parts of the brain are implicated[41].

Using post-mortem dissection, Bauman and Kemper found under-developed nerve cell bodies in the limbic system[42]. In 2001 Courchesne published a paper indicating that the autistic brain is characterised by overgrowth of neurons in the toddler years followed by unusually slow growth[43]. There is an abnormal increase in volume of gray matter in the cerebral areas and white matter in the cerebellum.

Behaviour can be related to the location of damage: in the frontal lobe areas it can result in an inability to make and carry out plans in daily life (Executive Function Theory)[44] and/or an inability to understand that other people may see

---

39   Jolliffe T, Lansdown R & Robinson C (1992) Autism: a personal account. *Communication* **26** 3. (Hard copies paper obtainable from the The National Autistic Society.)

40   Courchesne E, Yeung-Courchesne R, Press GA, Hesselink JR & Jernigan TL (1988) Hypoplasia of cerebellar vermal lobules VI and VII in autism. *New England Journal of Medicine* **318** (21) 1349–1354.

41   Takashima F and Matsuishi T (2017) *Autism as Seen from the Field of Neuroscience* (paper in preparation). Available at: matsuishi-lab.org/autismunderstanding-brainscienceJP_EN.htm (accessed September 2017).

42   Bauman ML & Kemper TL (2015*) The Neurobiology of Autism* (2nd edition). Baltimore: The John Hopkins University Press.

43   Courchesne E, Karns CM, Davis HR, Ziccardi R, Carper RA, Tigue ZD, Chisum HJ, Moses P, Pierce K, Lord C, Lincoln AJ, Pizzo S, Schreibman L, Haas RH, Akshoomoff NA & Courchesne RY (2001) Unusual brain growth patterns in early life in patients with autistic disorder: an MRI study. *Neurology* **57** (2) 245–254.

44   Happé F (1994) *Autism: An introduction to psychological theory*. London: University College London Press.

things differently (Theory of Mind)[45]. In addition, regions of the brain do not work in isolation but are parts of an interlocking network of information transfer. If one area is damaged it may well affect not just its immediate function but others that are linked to it. An excellent (and accessible) overview of somewhat contradictory current research is provided by Donovan and Basson[46]. They conclude that it is now, 'unlikely that one single neuroanatomical alteration or developmental abnormality will be found to underlie the majority of autism pathology' but suggest that genetic evidence points towards about ten autism subgroups (rather than the hundreds of genes that have been identified as associated with autism spectrum disorder).

For example, making the connection between neuroscience and behavioural dysfunction, speech difficulties are traditionally related to the Wernicke's area of the brain (usually the left temporal lobe: language comprehension) and Broca's area (left frontal: speech articulation and language production). However, recent research using fMRI scans suggests it is not simply a question of damage to one area of the brain or another, but rather the connections between them, so that these cannot 'talk' to each other. For example, autistic brains may find it difficult to analyse speech because they are unable to segment the unbroken flow of noise into words. This is a task that involves stimulating a connection between the two areas, which is difficult for people on the spectrum: 'When people with autism listen to a stream of syllables, there is no connection between these two major areas of the brain'[47]. Hence, in conversation, Donna Williams describes herself as, 'running, running, running, trying to keep up'.

Another area which is the focus of current research is the cerebellum, the spongy looking region sitting between the brain stem and lower rear part of the main brain. Traditionally it was thought that the cerebellum was only concerned with the coordination of muscles and the maintenance of bodily equilibrium. On balance, evidence now suggests that in addition to motor pathways, the cerebellum is also implicated in perceptual pathways, especially those which involve motor activity, such as eye movement and focus. The detail of how it is involved is currently being explored, so the language of research papers is speculative, couched in terms of 'maybe' and 'might'. Nevertheless, the possibilities are fascinating.

Coming down to the cellular level, the cerebellum is packed with Purkinje cells. Discovered as early as 1837 by the Czech anatomist Jan Evangelista Purkinje, they are like beautiful trees with multiple branched dendrites, forming what

45   Baron-Cohen S & Bolton P (1993) *Autism: The facts*. Oxford: Oxford University Press.

46   Donovan A & Basson MA (2017) The neuroanatomy of autism – a developmental perspective. *Journal of Anatomy*. DOI: 10.1111/joa.12542.

47   Deweerdt S (2010) *Connections Between Language Areas Impaired in Autism* [online]. Spectrum News. Available at: https://spectrumnews.org/news/connections-between-language-areas-impaired-in-autism/ (accessed September 2017).

is known as a dendritic arbor[48]. They play a pivotal role in processing incoming synaptic information and relaying it to multiple regions in the brain and spinal cord. In particular, they boost or moderate the level of incoming sensory signals. The evidence now is that in the autistic brain, the Purkinje cells are failing in their function of damping down the level of signals, and that this is related to a problem of not enough synaptic pruning[49]. The outcome is that the brain gets overwhelmed by too much irrelevant data, which we know as contributing to sensory overload[50].

Linked to this, another deficit that has been studied is a reduction in the number of Purkinje cells in the cerebellum in autistic people, which are involved in the transmission of messages from the eyes and ears to the visual processing area. This intimate coordination between hearing, vision and motor movement is demonstrated by an autistic child who told me that when her visual deficit is corrected using tinted lenses then she knows which way to point her head to pick up a sound[51].

Not only are the individual Purkinje cells failing to lower the level of stimuli, but also it has been shown that (in a limited number of post mortem studies) there was a shortage of Purkinje cells, with consequent competition for their pathways and hence scrambled transmission. These findings are supported by *in vivo* imaging, using diffusion MRI tractography[52]. In other words it is now possible to watch the reduced activity in the pathway from the sense organs to the brain, while it is happening in living people on the spectrum. The effect of this is that messages from the receptive organs are scrambled before a decision is made about possible responses.

Whether the pathways in the brain are over-connected, so that the brain is flooded with irrelevant information, or under-connected, there is an impediment to the free-flow of information from one area of the brain to another. In terms of

48   http://bridgeblog.scientopia.org/2011/09.26/a-neuroscience-field-guide-the-purkinje-cell/

49   'Synaptic pruning' refers to the cut-back of excess connections made between brain cells as children struggle to make sense of their environment. This takes place around the age of 2 ½ to 3 years. See also page 37.

50   Piochon C, Kloth AD, Grasselli G, Titley HK, Nakayama H, Hashimoto K, Wan V, Simmons DH, Eissa T, Nakatani J, Cherskov A, Miyazaki T, Watanabe M, Takumi T, Kano M, Wang SS-H & Hansel C (2014) Cerebellar plasticity and motor learning deficits in a copy-number variation mouse model of autism. *Nature Communications* 5 (5586) doi:10.1038/ncomms6586. Available at: https://www.nature.com/articles/ncomms6586 (accessed September 2017).

51   Personal communication.

52   Jeong-Won J, Tiwari VN, Behen HT & Chugani DC (2014) *In vivo* detection of reduced Purkinje cell fibers with diffusion MRI tractography in children with autistic spectrum disorders [online]. *Frontiers in Human Neuroscience* 8 (110). Available at: http://journal.frontiersin.org/article/10.3389/fnhum.2014.00110/full (accessed September 2017).

helping the individual to understand what is happening, there are both log-jams and gaps. What is more, the connectivity deficits are not consistent. Again using fMRI scanning, a particular visual stimulus evoked a consistent response in the brain in non-autistic controls. In the autistic brain, the responses were variable – 'in trial after trial, sometimes there was strong response and sometimes a weak response'[53].

Such inconsistencies may make it extremely difficult for the autistic brain to adapt to a deficit. It seems possible that the complaint expressed by unskilled support workers that, 'he's lazy, we know he can understand because sometimes he will do what we ask but sometimes will not' may relate to such variability. Maybe it is we who should look for better ways of conveying meaning. In the chapter on Responsive Communication (Chapter 13) I shall come back to possible ways of bypassing such stoppages.

---

53 Dinstein I, Heeger DJ, Lorenzi L, Minshew NJ, Malach R & Behrmann M (2012) Unreliable evoked responses in autism. *Neuron* **75** (6) 981–991.

Chapter 5: Historical interlude

By way of introduction to the corpus callosum and its vital role underpinning behavioural patterns in some people on the autistic spectrum, I want to have a brief word about its chequered history and the part played by the two halves of the brain and the fibres that join them.

As early as 470 BC, Hippocrates taught that the brain was the seat of intelligence and that the two halves of the brain were capable of independent processing. In particular he noted that paralysis occurs on the side of the body opposite to that of a brain injury (that is the right half of the brain controls the left half of the body and vice versa)[54]. Although there is some confusion about the teachings of Diocles of Carystus (a contemporary of Aristotle), it is thought that it was he who suggested:

'There are two brains in the head, one which gives us our intellect and another that provides sentience. That is, the one that lies on the right side is the one that senses; with the left one however, we understand.' [55]

His ideas, which could have been said today, seem to have been completely lost, but are important from the point of view of autism and understanding harmonious brain functioning, since the balance between the two halves of the brain and particularly their ability to communicate, is clearly disturbed in the brains of some people on the spectrum.

Following the Greeks, the actual function of the brain was a matter of speculation rather than investigation, since the human body was regarded as too sacred to be dissected. Such dissection as there was tended to be carried out on the brains of animals such as the Barbary ape.

Jumping to the Renaissance, Andreas Vesalius identified the corpus callosum joining the two halves of the brain[56]. But equally interesting from the point of view of our later discussions on self-awareness is an enigmatic 'double take' woodcut published in his book, *De Humani Corporis Fabrica* (1543).

---

54   http://schatz.sju.edu/neuro/nphistory/nphistory.html

55   Lokhorst G-JC (1985) Hemisphere differences before 1800. *Behavioural and Brain Sciences* **8** (4) 642.

56   http://neuroportraits.eu/portrait/andreas-vesalius

Easy to miss at first glance, focus on the whole rather than the detail. Vesalius has embedded a self-portrait of his head and shoulders in the brain as seen from below. His beard flows down over the cerebellum, which stands in for a ruff. While it has been suggested that the 'portrait' may have been a later addition superimposed by the printer, it is equally possible that it is part of the original, since, in a letter accompanying the first iteration of Fabrica, Vesalius warns Operinus, his printer, to remain faithful to the text and not to alter the smallest piece of the original[57]. Is Vesalius (well-known as a self-publicist) implying that the brain is the centre of self-awareness? This is where I am?

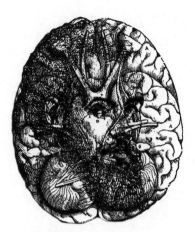

In 1780 Du Pui[58] writes that man is a 'homo duplex', with two distinct beings, a right man and a left one. Since then, the arguments as to the degree to which the two hemispheres act independently have drifted backwards and forwards. In the 1840s Arthur Wigan[59] offered the idea that we have 'a moral imperative to keep both hemispheres balanced, since if one becomes diseased or insane, the other can still control its morbid volitions'. If the left brain represents civilised and rational behaviour, the right brain embodies impulsivity, savagery, animality and madness – and is associated with so-called 'inferior groups', for example, women. Stevenson's 'Jekyll and Hyde'[60] germinates from this supposition.

Gradually speculation gave way to science. In the 1860s, Broca investigated the disappearance of speech in a man he knew called Tan. When Tan died, it was Broca who conducted his post-mortem. It emerged that Tan had had a lesion in the 'pars triangularis of the third left frontal convolution'. While alive he had been articulate and could write, but was unable to speak. Broca writes:

'What is lost therefore is not the faculty of language, is not the memory of words, nor the action of the nerves and muscles of phonation and articulation. It is a particular faculty to coordinate the movements that belong to articulate language; for without it no articulation is possible.'[61]

57   Carswell B *Andreas Vesalius' Fabrica: The Anatomy of a Revolution*. Available at: https://www. abebooks.com/rare-books/andreas-vesalius-fabrica.shtml (accessed September 2017).

58   Du Pui MS (1780) *De Homino Dextro et Sinistro*.

59   Wigan L (1844) *A New View of Insanity: The duality of the mind*. London: Longman, Brown, Green, and Longmans.

60   Stiles A (2012) *Popular Fiction and Brain Science in the Late Nineteenth Century*. Cambridge: Cambridge University Press.

61   Berker EA, Berker AH & Smith A (1986) Translation of Broca's 1865 report. Localisation of speech in the third left frontal convolution. *Archives of Neurology* **43** 1065-1072.

Meanwhile the idea that specific areas of the brain could be related to specific faculties was gathering strength. As far back as 1810 Gall had assigned numbers to individual gyri (the ridges between folds on the brain surface), linking each with a specific brain function. The notion that these might be detected as lumps on the skull gave birth to an army of Fowler's (always male) china heads divided into numbered, labelled or even pictorial areas, each relating to a specific attribute, such as, on the left: sublimity, cautiousness, acquisitiveness and destructiveness, with selfish sentiments, intuitive, reasoning and reflective capacities on the right, among many others. Round the neck of the replica above my desk is the following comment:

'For thirty years I have studied Crania and living heads from all parts of the world and have found in every instance there is a perfect correspondence between the conformation of an individual and his known characteristics. To make my observations available I have prepared a bust of superior form and marked the divisions of the organs in accordance with my researches and varied experience. Signed, L.N. Fowler.'

Scrambling to keep up with evolving ideas, as late as 1916 Fowler's 'New Phrenological Bust' was still being advertised as a teaching aid – 'newly discovered organs are added and old organs have been subdivided to indicate the various phases of action which many of them assume'[62]. The idea that character could be read by feeling the bumps of the skull took hold of public imagination. They still hold a somewhat creepy fascination.

As a way of reading character, feeling the bumps turned out to be a blind alley, but one with a small window at the far end. Although phrenology was incorrect, 'its impact was sufficient to direct neurological interest towards nerve function rather than dwelling on the concept of an insubstantial soul'[63].

But by now the intellectual cat was out of the bag. The microscope was in common use and new staining methods had been devised. Santiago Ramon y Cajal discovered the neuron (nerve cell) as a basic unit of the brain, with subsequent demonstration of their electrical excitability and their ability to affect the electrical charge of adjacent neurons[64].

Nowadays, increasingly sophisticated scanners monitor our glucose metabolism, blood flow and oxygen uptake. We are able to watch identifiable parts of the brain

---

62   Clarke E & Dewhurst K (1974) *An Illustrated History of Brain Function.* Los Angeles: University of California Press.

63   Ibid.

64   Wikipedia: http://en.wikipedia.org/wiki/History_of_neuroscience

in action while they perform specific actions. We can begin to assign particular functions to specific cranial activity. For example, brain scans of Temple Grandin, who is autistic and famous for her phenomenal capacity to visualise elaborate cattle pens and engineering structures down to the last screw without having to draw up blueprints, show an overdeveloped grouping of fibres in her visual area and a rather disorganised speech processing area[65].

Transcranial magnetic stimulation suggests that the classic view of Wernicke's area as concerned only with speech decoding and Broca's area as being where speech is produced, is oversimplified: other parts of the brain are involved and may even differ from person-to-person. (The same is also true for visual processing where up to thirty different modules may be involved, for example, one that exclusively defines edges.) Using what is known as the 'connectionist model'[66] whereby different aspects of language are managed by distinct modules in the brain, it is becoming clear that it is the linkages between them which are critical – and language disorders arise from breakdowns in connections between these modules.

A far cry from the idea that the brain is composed of undifferentiated phlegm, Liebermann summarises the contemporary role of the brain, linking its experience of the outside world with its architecture:

'The brain is an interface between the ethereal and the organic, where feelings and memories composing the ineffable fabric of experience are transmuted into molecular biochemistry.' [67]

All of us have brains that develop differently. We are neither clones nor drones, we have various strengths and weaknesses, not just cognitively but affectively. Even identical twins are different people. These differences are just as evident when it comes to autism. Not only is the individual unique, but so also are the areas of developmental impairment. There is no 'standard model for' any of us.

---

65 Grandin T (2014) *The Autistic Brain*. London: Rider Books.

66 Geschwind N (1970) The organization of language and the brain. *Science* **170** (3961) pp. 940–944.

67 Liebermann JA (2015) *Shrinks: The untold story of psychiatry*. London: Weidenfield and Nicolson.

Chapter 6: Two brains

The brains of people with autism have developed differently from those who are not on the spectrum. Just as the rest of us are different, so are individuals with autism, but on top of this, the developmental differences are not the same in each individual. There is no standard model.

This month I was asked to visit six different children at one school whose particular difficulties were manifest in completely different ways. Two had problems with hypersensitivities (one light, one sound), another had experienced trauma, another had no sight and part of the brain had not developed and so on. Like the rest of us, some were very able and some were so restricted by their deficits that they were less able. Although the variety of behaviours they presented was very wide ranging, all were diagnosed with autism. In this chapter I want to look at investigations into the nature of the two halves of the brain and how this may throw light on the behaviour of some people with autism.

Used as we are to the idea of one creature, one brain, not all creatures have evolved the same arrangement. For example, although humans and octopuses have a common worm-like ancestor that lived 750 million years ago, octopus brains have evolved differently, with a central command station that issues an overall instruction, which then feeds into eight sub-stations; bundles of neurons, one in each of its arms. So each arm is capable of independent reflex actions. If the central brain spots prey, it sends out a general message of 'eat' and the arms issue necessary motor signals independently. They can even recoil from unpleasant stimuli after detachment from the main body. Some cephalopods (squid and octopus) will actually shed a limb in the face of threat, which thrashes round as a distraction in order for the main body to escape its predator in much the same way as the severed tails of an earthworm. They then grow a replacement. This shedding must happen quite often as they often have arms of different lengths, presumably in different stages of regeneration[68].

Despite the human brain's unpromising appearance, its apparent inertia is deceptive. Even when we think it is at rest, it is hard at work. Raichle *et al* used PET scanners to compare brain activity when doing a task (such as watching shapes on a computer) with the resting state when the eyes are closed. They were surprised to find that the level of brain activity actually drops when the brain switches from the passive to an active state[69]. To put it another way, it was

---

68   Courage KH (2013) Even severed octopus arms have smart moves. *Scientific American* **27 August.**

69   Raichle ME, Macleod AM, Snyder AZ, Powers WJ, Gusnard DA & Shulman Gl (2001) A default mode of brain function. *PNAS* **98** (2) 676–682.

working harder when it was apparently doing nothing, than when it was active. They named this state of passive activity, 'The Default Network'. This default network switches on (consuming vast quantities of glucose) when we 'switch off'. The suggestion is that when it is not engaged in 'work', areas of the brain such as medial prefrontal cortex, chatter to the hippocampus (involved in memory). Instead of doing nothing, the brain is busy integrating what it has learned into plans for the future – and sorting out positive from negative memories; a kind of selective housekeeping that prevents the build-up of irrelevant (and in some cases harmful) clutter, clogging up the works. The authors suggest that, rather than being broken down to provide energy, unwanted glucose is incorporated into amino acids to provide building blocks, which are built into neurotransmitters to maintain and synthesise the new synapses involved in memory[70]. Interestingly, the activity of the default system is more pronounced when its chatter relates to personal self rather than other than self. And it appears that there is disruption to the default system, not only in Alzheimer's but also in ADHD and autism. Presumably, if the sensory clutter is not being sifted out, it builds up to become yet another log-jam in the processing system.

Looking at the human brain we see one brain: so why two halves? What are they doing? Are they supporting each other or in competition? Do they specialise? Is one side dominant as was once thought – and does this affect the way a person thinks and behaves? What happens when the two halves cannot talk to each other?

To begin with, the 'wiring' is odd, with a neural crossover behind the eyes. The right hand brain deals with the left half of the body (and information from the left field of vision), while the left hand brain commands the right half of the body. So, incoming information from the left hand field of vision is processed by the right hemisphere and vice versa – information from the right hand field of vision ends up in the left half of the brain. In actual fact, the crossover, which takes place behind the eyes (at the optic chiasm) is not the whole process. During development in the embryo, nerve cell axons (the long thread-like extensions of nerves that carry messages to the short branched receptors – dendrites – of adjacent nerves), grow out from the retina at the back of the eyes, towards the brain and most of them make the crossing at mid-line, but some are redirected and turn back, so that they feed into their original hemisphere. Controlled by a gene, Zic2, this diversion leads to the situation where an object is viewed through two different sittings, which gives us binocular vision. Implicated also in bilateral development of the brain, if this gene fails early on, such failure not only interferes with the ability to be able to detect the distance of objects, but on rare occasion produces a brain that is itself undivided into two halves.

---

70   Fox D (2013) Secret life of the brain. In: J Webb (Ed) *Nothing: Surprising insights everywhere from zero to oblivion*. London: Profile Books Ltd.

It is important to realise that during development everything is on the move; cells reach out, sliding over one another and linking up, laying down pathways between the various processing modules of the brain. During the early development of the brain, so urgent is this need for neurons to plug into each other that the outcome is over-connectivity, a state that as we have seen, requires selective pruning of the weaker synapses at a later stage, cutting back on links that are unused.

Autistic or not, in the first few years of our lives we are desperate to make sense of the world into which we have been born and we make far too many connections (synapses) between the nerve cells.

As the brain matures, special cells known as microglial cells cut back unused connections. Glial cells, whose activities are not yet fully understood, seem to act as the service industry of the brain, performing a multitude of functions, but are not involved in message transmission. In this case, they trim away unused connections between nerve cells during brain maturation, a process known as synaptic pruning[71]. Failure in the pruning process leads to an excess of connections and presumably the chaos that ensues, described by an autistic woman as 'like having a Molotov cocktail exploding in my head'[72]. One way or another, failure in this trimming process can lead to pathways that are over-connected, under-connected and cross-connected, or in some cases missing altogether.

Cx3cr1 is the gene that controls microglia production. Where it has been deleted in 'autistic model' mice, so that there is a deficiency in microglia (and therefore too many connections, or weaker connections), this is sufficient to promote autistic-related behaviour, such as repetitive behaviours and social unresponsiveness[73]. To put it the other way round, repetitive behaviour ('stimming') can be related to not enough pruning of excess synapses, although this may not be directly causal, in other words stimming arises as a way of dealing with the consequences of too many connections. Combining with failure of the default system to clear up what Donna Williams has described as 'garbage', this over-connectivity results in the information overload and chaotic sensory experience that so many people on the spectrum describe[74]. The processing chaos resulting from visual sensory overload can clearly be seen in SPECT scans (Single Proton Emission Computed Tomography) which compare brain activity in the same child doing the same task.

---

71 Tang G, Gudsnuk K, Kuo SH, Cotrina ML, Rosoklija G, Sosunov A, Sonders MS, Kanter E, Castagna C, Yamamoto A, Yue Z, Arancio O, Peterson BS, Champagne F, Dwork AJ, Goldman J, & Sulzer D (2014) Loss of mTOR-dependent macroautophagy causes autistic-like synaptic pruning deficits. *Neuron* **83** (5) 1131–1143.

72 Personal communication.

73 Zhan Y, Paolicelli RC, Sforazzini F, Weinhard L, Bolasco G, Pagani F, Vyssotski AL, Bifone A, Gozzi A, Ragozzino D & Gross CT (2014) Deficient neuron-microglia signaling results in impaired functional brain connectivity and social behavior. *Nature Neuroscience* **17** (3) 400–406.

74 Irlen H (2010) *The Irlen Revolution*. New York: Square One Publishers.

Such sensitivities to sensory overload can lead to social avoidance in order to cut down on incoming stimuli, since the sounds people make, their bright clothes and constant movement and demands overwhelm the processing system. Too many connections and everything just keeps firing off at once. So there is a tendency for people the spectrum to focus on one object (fixation), or activity (stimming), in order to cut out the unmanageable sensory overload and the anxiety this triggers.

As was pointed out earlier, when Kavee flips endlessly though his iPad, he is not trying to pick out any particular program, but doing this because when he swipes it, it moves: he gets a response that he can control. In a world of sensory chaos there is at least one activity in his life that is predictable. When people are self-stimulating, what they are actually trying to do is to 'self-generate' markers to identify a safe space to protect themselves from sensory overload and anxiety.

Unsurprisingly, research confirms the link between level of anxiety and increasing focus on repetitive behaviours[75]. Unless we listen to what people with autism are telling us about their condition we may fall into the trap of attributing behaviour (that is at least in part a reaction to sensory hyper or hyposensitivity and at least potentially can be corrected), to some deficit in personality.

Synaptic pruning shapes the direction of pathways between different areas of the brain: taking a wrong turning can result, for example, in synaesthesia, where one sense is processed as a different sense.

Synaesthesia is a condition more frequently found in people on the autistic spectrum than in the normal population. On the other hand, abundant cross wiring is also linked to the creative capacity characteristic of artists, poets and writers, facilitating metaphorical thinking, linking ideas in unusual ways[76]. The more that is learned about these unusual paths of neuro-development and their consequent behaviour patterns, the more that many are being traced back to gene fragilities of one sort or another. And these aberrations can be either inherited or the result of environmental hazards.

Although we humans can manage if one half of the brain (or the connection between the two of them) is damaged, unusual connectivity can be related to differences in behaviour and cognitive ability, not necessarily negative. As an extreme example, the post-mortem examination of Einstein's brain removed

---

75 Rodgers J, Riby DM, Janes EJ, Connolly B & McConachie H (2012) Anxiety and repetitive behaviours in autism spectrum disorders and williams syndrome: a cross-syndrome comparison. *Journal of Autism and Developmental Disorders* **42** (2) 175.

76 Ramachandran VS (2007) *Three Clues to Understanding your Brain*. Ted Talk. Available at: https://www.youtube.com/watch?v=Rl2LwnaUA-k (accessed September 2017).

eight days after he died, revealed unusually thickened connections between the parts involved in abstract thinking and decision making (the prefrontal cortex), the areas involved in sense and motor function (the parietal lobe) and his visual cortex. It is suggested that Einstein's genius may have been at least partly related to this enhanced connectivity.

On the other hand, although the sample numbers are small, up to one third of children with deficits in the corpus callosum, the bridge between the two halves of the brain, have problems that are also associated with autism, such as coping with the secondary meanings of language[77]. They struggle to understand things like jokes, sarcasm and figures of speech[78]. The expression 'raining stair rods' would be taken literally.

So can we find out what the outcome is when the two halves are separated? Most investigations into what happens if there is interference between the two hemispheres have been prompted by surgery on the corpus callosum in patients with epilepsy, physically separating the two halves in order to reduce the effect of severe seizures that are not responding to other treatments. In the opening chapter we met Jill Bolte Taylor, who had a stroke in her thirties and as a result lost her memory and her ability to walk, talk, read or write. In affective terms, her left brain was flooded and the two halves of her brain were cut off from each other, as they might have been if it had been her corpus callosum that had been damaged. What she was left with was her right hand brain. As mentioned in the introduction, eight years later, and now fully recovered, her experience offers a unique combination of an insider's view of a rare brain haemorrhage – coupled with her neurological observations and understanding of what was happening to her[79].

Although it is no longer believed that which hemisphere is dominant determines whether we are 'thinking' or 'feeling' people, each side has its own way of processing information. Jill gives us an overview of the characteristics of the two different hemispheres, since she has been deeply involved not only in research but through her personal experience which she is sharing with the world. This is important because we need to marry the outside-in point of view, which focuses on empirical data, with the inside-out perspective which is concerned with qualitative experience. Current research tends to focus on the former at the expense of the latter.

---

77 De Weerdt S (2013) *Lack of Corpus Callosum Yields Insights into Autism*. SFARI Simons Foundation Autism Research Initiative, 2 May 2013.

78 Paul LK, Van Lancker-Sidtis D, Schieffer B, Dietrich R & Brown WS (2003) Communicative deficits in agenesis of the corpus callosum: nonliteral language and affective prosody. *Brain and Language* **85** (2) 313–324.

79 Bolte Taylor J (2009) *My Stroke of Insight: A brain scientist's personal journey*. London: Hodder & Stoughton.

Drawing on an analogy of the computer, we are told that processing of data in the right hemisphere is in parallel, whereas left hemisphere processing is linear. For the non IT-minded, a simple image is like the arrival in the right hemisphere of a patrol of soldiers marching line abreast. In the left hemisphere, the patrol is marching in single file[80]. The affect is that in the right hemisphere all the information arrives simultaneously, or, as Jill puts it, bursting into a collage of sensory experience of the present moment.

In both her film and her book, as her left hemisphere ceases to function, Jill explains:

'Moments don't come and go in a rush but rather are rich with sensations, thought, emotions and often, physiological responses. Information gathered this way allows us to take an immediate inventory about the space around us and our relationship to that space….borders between specific entities are softened…to our right mind, the moment of now is timeless and abundant. ..'

'Our right mind thinks intuitively outside the box…everything and every one are connected together as one…. our ability to be empathetic is a product of the right cerebral hemisphere.' [81]

In the left hemisphere, just as the troops come in single file, information is processed more slowly, waiting for all the relevant data packages to arrive, placing them in context of the past and future. This is where detail is considered, time is born and our moments are divided into past, present and future. One half of the brain is the artist seeing the landscape as a whole, the other is the town-planner, chewing over details, granting or refusing permissions to build.

As a speaker, consciously or unconsciously (perhaps both), Jill's body language during the film is remarkable. She holds a human brain with its (to the layman somewhat unattractive) dangling spinal cord in the palms of her hands with reverence, almost awe. And as she describes the workings of the two halves – and particularly their behaviour during the four hours her stroke lasted before she lost consciousness – her facial expression and posture alter radically. Two different characters: as she describes it, the 'we' that lives in 'me'. And as one might expect, when she is describing being in her left hemisphere, her body language is that of a self-contained independent individual, whereas when she speaks of being in the right hemisphere and says she feels like a genie liberated from her bottle: she uses sweeping inclusive gestures that are an invitation to communicate and relate. In this mode she envisages a world 'filled with beautiful,

---

80   Metaphor supplied by Simon Whillan, with grateful thanks.

81   Bolte Taylor J (2008) *My Stroke of Insight*. Ted Talk. Available at: https://www.ted.com/talks/ jill_bolte_taylor_s_powerful_stroke_of_insight (accessed September 2017).

compassionate, loving people who knew they could come to this space at any time, that they could purposely choose to step to the right of their left hemisphere to find this peace...'

We shall return to a more detailed examination of Jill's journey through her right hemisphere in order to compare it with Donna Williams' reports of the inner world of autism, but, when we come to it, we shall need to remember that Donna herself warns us that she is not a spokesperson for everyone with autism; each person is different and we need to learn from that individual what has meaning for them.

As we turn our attention to the meticulous experimental work of Michael Gazzaniga and his team on surgery to individuals with severe epilepsy, their 'styles' are so different that it is important to remember that Jill is also a scientist, trained at Harvard University, a neuroanatomist, researching brain structure. At times her account feels evangelical, almost a conversion experience. Perhaps this is part of how a conversion experience might be experienced – as a profound entrance into the unbounded sensory affective world of the right hemisphere. But because her descriptions are so vivid and in a sense boundless, we need to understand that these are not the wild imaginings of a brain that had taken the bit between its teeth and galloped over the horizon, but an accurate record of her perceptions during the traumatic period of her stroke; what she observed and what she felt, and of the affect it has had on her sensory perception.

One of the amazing advances in the spread of information is that we can now attend lectures and listen to experts talk about their work on the internet. Via TED Talks we can watch live research happen in front of our eyes. As we follow their arguments we are caught up in the speaker's enthusiasm. In contrast to Jill's 'inside-out' experience, a remarkable film by Michael Gazzaniga, *Severed Corpus Callosum*, introduces us to his in-depth research. His is definitely an 'outside-in' approach. Although the two viewpoints are not irreconcilable, they are couched in very different language and different ways of looking at the same landscape. What they share is enthusiasm for the depth of their insight. Ultimately they reach the same conclusion: to work optimally, both halves of the brain need to communicate with each other; one tempers the other, and if it is internal (although as we shall see it is possible under exceptional circumstances to use external cueing), this link is normally routed through the corpus callosum.

Michael Gazzaniga has spent forty years working with patients whose epilepsy proved to be unmanageable. In order to limit the spread of frequent seizures they underwent surgery to sever the corpus callosum and were left with what appeared to be two independent brains. To the outsider his investigations are both breathtakingly simple and sophisticated.

A word of warning, for those of us who are vaguely ambidextrous and do not have a strong unconscious awareness of rightness or leftness, descriptions of these experiments are quite difficult to follow. This is for two reasons. Firstly, rather than instinctively 'knowing' which is left or which is right, we have to make a conscious effort to think about which is which. This slows up the process of differentiation, since conscious processing is about four hundred milliseconds slower than unconscious processing, a sort of tripwire in the flow of thought. Secondly, the expression, 'right hand brain' and 'left hand brain' compromises our ability to follow descriptions, since our right hand feeds information to the left hemisphere and vice versa. The clues are confusing: it is easy to end up chasing one's conceptual tail, so I shall stick to 'right hemisphere' and 'left hemisphere'.

Previous to surgery, Joe had been plagued by several severe epileptic seizures a day. Following the operation to separate the two halves of his brain, he is now able to lead a reasonably normal working life[82]. The essence of Gazzaniga's investigations were to focus Joe's attention to one side of a screen (therefore feeding the opposite brain with a word or image) and so tease out which half of his brain was picking up words, which dealt with images and which with emotions.

In an early experiment, Joe was looking at a screen, focusing on a cross in the middle of it. Anything flashed to the right of the cross went to his left brain and conversely, anything flashed to the left of the cross went to the right hemisphere. When the word 'PHONE' came up on his right screen and travelled to his left hemisphere, he immediately said the word 'phone'. But when a word was flashed on the left side of the screen and went to his right hemisphere, he said he cannot see it. But when he was asked to draw what came up on the left screen he drew the phone with his left hand (he had seen it but couldn't organise the sequences and muscular movements necessary to articulate the word). Astonishingly, once he could see what he had drawn, he could say what it was. So as Michael pointed out, Joe's ability to speak was lodged in the left hemisphere. When the word came up on the left hand of the screen and travelled to the right brain, Joe could only say it once he had drawn it – so in his case, communication was not directly between the two hemispheres but outside the brain through the paper on the desk in front of him. That is, since the bridge between the hemispheres had been surgically interrupted, he was using an external clue to make sense of what had failed to pass from his right brain to his left. In terms of autism, this idea is important in terms of possible therapeutic approaches. We shall return to this later.

Gazzaniga's experiments grew in complexity. Joe was then shown a screen with a snow-scene picture of a house on the left side (going to his right hemisphere)

---

82 Gazzaniga M. *Severed Corpus Callosum*. Available at: www.youtube.com/watch?v=RFgtGIL7vEY (accessed September 2017).

and a picture of a chicken claw on the right hand side (travelling to his left hemisphere). Below the screen were eight pictures which he was asked to relate to those on the screen. With his right hand, he pointed to a picture of a hen on the right, relating to the chicken claw, which he had seen in his left hemisphere. Dictated by his right non-speaking brain, he picked out a shovel on the left (relating to the snow scene). Remembering that there is no connection in Joe's brain between the right non-verbal half (which has seen the snow scene but cannot put it into words) and the verbal left half, when asked to say why he picked the shovel, instead of saying 'the shovel is to clear the snow', he said, 'that's simple, it's to shovel up the chicken shit'. When Joe's brain cannot explain why it has made a choice, it makes up a story to cover the facts as it perceives them. Enter the left brain 'interpreter', which is trying to concoct a coherent story to cover the facts (those that are at the disposal of his brain).

In another experiment, Gazzaniga demonstrates that recognition of faces is a skill of the right hemisphere. He showed Joe the strange paintings by the renaissance artist Archimboldo. These surreal portraits are made up of assembled fruit, vegetables, flowers or books. Flashed to the left screen (going to the right hemisphere), he was asked to point to one of two descriptive words, FACE or FRUIT – and pointed to the word FACE. He was seeing the whole. But when the picture came up on the right screen (travelling to the left hemisphere), Joe picked out the word FRUIT. So, rather than the complete picture, the left hemisphere is picking up on the detail from which it is assembled.

In the next chapter I shall be comparing Jill's and Donna's descriptions of the lure of the inner world unhindered by the critical evaluation of the interpreter.

Chapter 7: The bridge

Neurobiological research is challenging the way that we think about autism, pointing away from the consideration of its symptoms, such as the 'triad of impairments', to the underlying aetiology. The more that is learned about the spectrum, the stranger it seems that it is still being thought of (and treated) as a behavioural dysfunction rather than a neurological snarl-up.

Officially: 'Autism is a polygenetic developmental neurobiologic disorder with multiorgan involvement, though it predominantly involves central nervous system dysfunction…in particular, it is a disorder of connectivity'[83]. The latest figures issued by the Centres for Disease Control and Prevention (CDC) estimate that one in 68 children (or 14.7 per 1,000 eight-year-olds) in multiple communities in the United States have been identified with autism spectrum disorder (ASD)[84]. This figure compares with one in a 100 in Britain, the difference being accounted for by the stricter criteria used to define autism in the UK. Surprisingly, since it was thought previously that most cases were genetic in origin, a new study from the data of 2 million children born in Sweden between 1982 and 2006 suggests that as many as 50% are caused by environmental factors[85].

Whether acquired genetically or through contact with environmental hazard, the normal pattern of development is damaged. Gene sequences are duplicated or missed out – and these fragile templates lay the foundation for what is, at least potentially, neurobiological catastrophe. The whole system of nerve development and organ connectivity can be disrupted.

One aspect of this is the link between damage to the corpus callosum and autism spectrum disorder – up to one-third of individuals missing all, or part of the corpus callosum, meet the diagnostic criteria for autism[86]. Looking at it from the other way round, fMRI studies indicate that cortical under-connectivity and abnormal morphology of the corpus callosum is characteristic of individuals on

---

83   Minshew NJ & Williams DL (2007) The new neurobiology of autism: cortex, connectivity, and neuronal organization. *Archives of Neurology* **64** (7) 945–950.

84   Centers for Disease Control and Prevention (2014) Prevalence of Autism Spectrum Disorder among Children Aged 8 Years – Autism and Developmental Disabilities Monitoring Network, 11 Sites, United States, 2010. *Morbidity and Mortality Weekly Report* **63** (2).

85   Sandin S, Lichtenstein P, Kuja-Halkola R, Larsson H, Hultman CM & Reichenberg A (2014) The familial risk of autism. *Journal of the American Medical Association* **311** (17) 1770-1777.

86   DeWeerdt S (2013) *Lack of Corpus Callosum Yields Insights into Autism* [online]. Spectrum News. Available at: https://spectrumnews.org/news/lack-of-corpus-callosum-yields-insights-into-autism/ (accessed September 2017).

the autistic spectrum. 'An under-connected system would be particularly disruptive to those complex or higher order psychological functions with a heavy dependence on the coordination of brain regions, such as social, language and problem solving function'[87], leading to deficits in theory of mind,[88] face processing,[89] executive function[90] and language[91]. In other words, the left brain may not know what the right brain is doing or how to do it.

The brain activation of a group of high-functioning autistic participants was measured using fMRI during the performance of a Tower of London task, in comparison to a control group matched with respect to IQ, age, and gender. The two groups generally activated the same cortical areas to similar degrees. However, there were three indications of underconnectivity in the group with autism. First, the degree of synchronisation (i.e. the functional connectivity, or the correlation of the time series of the activation) between the frontal and parietal areas of activation was lower for the autistic than the control participants. Second, relevant parts of the corpus callosum, through which many of the bilaterally activated cortical areas communicate, were smaller in cross-sectional area in the autistic participants. Third, within the autism group but not within the control group, the size of the genu of the corpus callosum was correlated with frontal-parietal functional connectivity. These findings suggest that the neural basis of altered cognition in autism entails a lower degree of integration of information across certain cortical areas resulting from reduced intra-cortical connectivity. The results add support to a new theory of cortical underconnectivity in autism, which posits a deficit in integration of information at the neural and cognitive levels.

We grow from a formless blob to a differentiated adult and, autistic or not, it all goes back to our genes. They are in charge of how we develop. Progressively, our genes 'switch on' proteins which direct information to potential sites and are responsible for the layout and execution of the master plan.

There are many factors involved in the development of autism, but during the switching on cascade, if a particular gene does not switch on in a particular cell, the fate of the system that derives from it is compromised. It may not divide the right

87   Just MA, Cherkassky VL, Keller TA, Kana K & Minshew NJ (2007) Functional and anatomical cortical underconnectivity in autism: evidence from an fMRI study of an executive function task and corpus callosum morphometry. *Cerebral Cortex* **17** (4) 951–961.

88   Baron Cohen S, Leslie AM & Frith U (1985) Does the autistic child have a Theory of Mind? *Cognition* **21** 37–46.

89   Pierce K, Müller RA, Ambrose J, Allen G & Courchesne E (2001) Face processing takes place outside the fusiform 'face area' in autism: evidence from functional MRI'. *Brain* **124** (10) 2059–2073.

90   Ozonoff S, Pennington BF & Rogers SJ (1991) Executive functioning deficits in high-functioning autistic individuals: relationship to theory of mind. *Journal of Child Psychology and Psychiatry* **32** (7) 1081–1105.

91   Just MA, Cherkassky VL, Keller TA & Minshew NJ (2004) Cortical activation and synchronisation during sentence comprehension in high functioning autism. *Brain* **127** (8) 1811–1821.

number of times, may not grow the right number of branches, or move into the right place, or it may die. If the cells make the wrong connections or fail to grow, sensory information will not reach from one part of the brain to another. Or if they overgrow, it will be like trying to listen to the radio through static. And possibly both.

But what does it feel like to live in this different and sensorily chaotic parallel world? How is it experienced?

While comparisons of states of sensory sensation may be suspect (since the same sensation may arise from different sources), it does seem legitimate to return to Jill Bolte Taylor's history of her sensory loss when her left brain haemorrhaged, and compare this with self-advocate accounts from the autistic spectrum. Where this is the case, both involve a loss of connection between the two halves of the brain and to do so throws light on what separation of the hemispheres involves in affective terms. But while accounts from autism highlight remarkable similarities there may also be a very different outcome, as will become apparent.

We now have extensive descriptions of the inside-out view of autistic experience and these certainly tie in to the probability that they have damaged connections between their right and left hemispheres. Those on the spectrum describe the difficulties experienced as lack of boundaries, the problems that they have with speech and their hypersensitivities to both external sensations such as light and sound as well as internal sensations such as the feeling of embarrassment due to emotional overload.

In spite of striking similarities, Jill's experience of losing contact with her left hemisphere – tranquil euphoria – contrasts strongly with descriptions from the autistic spectrum. Donna reminds us that experience of her inner world can be a frightening trip.

Jill offers us a clue to this divergence:

'How fortunate that the part of my brain that registered fear (my amygdala), had not reacted with alarm to these unusual circumstances and shifted me into a state of panic. As my language centres in my left hemisphere shut down and I became detached from the memories of my life, I was comforted by an expanding sense of grace.'[92]

Whether the experience is viewed as positive or negative is dependent on the setting of the amygdala, which acts as a sorting gate that can open either way into a positive or negative experience. Which way it swings will be dependent

---

92   Bolte Taylor J (2009) *My Stroke of Insight: A brain scientist's personal journey*. London: Hodder & Stoughton, p41.

on the threshold at which the amygdala is triggered by fear. In autistic people it would appear that the autonomic nervous system is so easily aroused by a trigger-happy amygdala that they may be locked into anxiety and fear: this is their first response, even to life events that are user-friendly to the non-autistic world. Jolliffe tells us of the terror she lives in all the time[93].

Jill's oceanic loss of boundaries reads very differently to those – frequently described but underreported – of people with autism. In spite of the pain she was experiencing, hers was a peaceful and all embracing experience.

Wearing her neuroanatomist hat, Jill presents us with a picture of the brain in which the two left and right hemispheres complement each other, telling us who we are and what we are doing.

'Cells in the left hemisphere's orientation association area define the boundaries of our body, where we begin and where we end relative to the space around us. At the same time there are cells in our right hemisphere orientation association area that orientate our body in space. As a result our left hemisphere tells us where our body begins and ends and our right hemisphere helps us place it where it wants to go'.[94]

As her left hand brain fades, she says, 'I could no longer discern the boundaries of where I began and where I ended. Instead I now blended with the space and flow around me'.

Both Jill and Donna speak of the lure of the inner world but in different terms. Jill calls it seductive. She turns inwards from what she now perceives as the insignificant demands of society. Her 'consciousness slowed to a soothing and satisfying awareness of the vast and wondrous world within'. She felt in a state of grace, ethereal. In full flight from sensory overload, Donna also talks about 'the hypnotism of it, the grip' and the 'grab' of a place where the whole world is made redundant as you have every relationship with yourself that you could have with people in the world and they don't matter any more'. While Jill describes her inner space as inclusive, for Donna it is exclusive; a prison rather than Nirvana. And Donna adds ominously, 'all right if you can visit it but if you have to live there, you live there in fear'. Turning now from a loss of boundaries, to the ability to speak. First Jill[95], again speaking as a scientist:

---

93   Jolliffe T, Lansdown R & Robinson C (1992) Autism: A personal account. *Communication* **26** 3. (Hard copies paper obtainable from the The National Autistic Society.

94   Bolte Taylor J (2009) *My Stroke of Insight: A brain scientist's personal journey.* London: Hodder & Stoughton.

95   Ibid.

'Although each of our cerebral hemispheres process information in uniquely different ways, the two work intimately with one another. With language for example, our left hemisphere understands the details making up the structure and semantics of the sentence – and the meaning of the words. It is our left mind that understands what letters are and how they fit together to create a sound (word) that has a concept (meaning) attached to it. It then strings the words together in a linear fashion to create sentences and paragraphs capable of delivering very complex messages. Our right hemisphere complements the action of the left hemisphere by interpreting non-verbal communication. It evaluates the more subtle cues of language including tone of voice, facial expression and body language. Inconsistencies may indicate someone is lying. Without the right hemisphere's ability to evaluate communication in the context of the bigger picture the left hemisphere tends to interpret everything literally.'

Compare this with a film illustrating Donna's struggles to express herself which she illustrates with the aid of some model cows[96]. (In this respect it is interesting that she was unable to talk about her expressive difficulties until a friend suggested that she used models to make her point. She had to feel and see them before she could articulate her problems.) As Gazzaniga pointed out in his research with Joe in the previous chapter, the connection between what Donna's brain knew but could not articulate needed to be made outside the brain, or in this case, in a mode that did not involve interpretation. The connection was made by external cueing through seeing and feeling. (I am quoting this in full since it illustrates so graphically the difficulties she experienced in the processing of speech, not just what she said but how she expressed it.)

'A lot of people think that there's only one way of processing but I think there's all different ways of thinking. And I think if you had [two] people, she picks up two cows to illustrate this, you look and say, oh yeah, that's a person and that's a person and you assume that they've got the same kind of thinking. But if this is the non-autistic person [a large black and white bull], the information comes into them and they can walk through life at a reasonable pace and take in information and spit it back out. [All this time she is moving the cows around to illustrate what she is sayin]. And this one I'll maybe call an autistic person [she loads his back with some strips of Blue-tack], he's kind of a bit wobbly [she nudges the cow so it falls over]. And it's not so easy, sometimes he can like, deal with the information and sometimes he can't because it's too many different channels coming in all at once. And this one [the autistic one] maybe not go further and think, "oh yes that equals table" and maybe not go further and think, "oh yeah that's for putting the things on". So then this [the non-autistic one] lives in the same world as this one and when they look at each other they sometimes don't see it all the same.

---

96   Williams D (1996) *Jam-Jar*. Channel 4 programme. Glasgow: Fresh Film & Television.

So this one, [the non-autistic person], *says, "Go and put the dinner on the table" and it is just all sounds because to him* [the autistic one] *he's weighed down by this'* [sensory overload represented by the lump of Blue-tack]. *He doesn't always quickly make the sounds into words and then the words into pictures and the pictures into the doing. For him it's not just all like that for his thinking reality. So maybe the non-autistic one says, "Go and put the dinner on the table" and the autistic person just stands there. So he says "take the plate to the table" and he's just holding the plate. So the non-autistic one says, You must be stupid, you're not intelligent. I learned the different sounds the things made, I learned the different textures the things made, I learned the different sound backs* [echoes] *that told me if they had bounce,* [she bangs the cow on the table] *if they didn't the impact that came back to you. That was what I called the "system of sensing". So I didn't need to interpret and interpretation was redundant, so all the world of words is part of the system of interpretation. But then they kept insisting that I answer them with words. "Answer me when I speak to you, go and do this, come and do that" and always trying to make me go in a system that involves making meaning all the time. And this created in me a war so I decided that the only safe place was inside my self, because all this* [she jerks the autistic cow aggressively towards the bull] *was foreign and invading.'*

Donna's support worker is wrong. Rather than unintelligent, she is exceptionally clever and creative. An artist and musician, she speaks four languages. She has written many books, her first three together are the most comprehensive of all accounts to shed light on the inner world of autism[97]. When she was struggling with language, what she was doing with her 'system of sensing' was building up a dictionary of sensory experiences. But this way of coding the sensory words does make generalisation difficult.

I have quoted Jill's and Donna's rather long excerpts in full because they throw considerable light on each other. Donna's account tallies almost exactly with the difficulties that Jill describes with the organisation and production of language in her disabled left hemisphere.

---

97   Williams D *Nobody Nowhere, Somebody Somewhere and Autism: An Inside Out Approach.*

Table 1. Effects of left hemisphere brain damage				
	Brain undamaged (Gazziniga)	**Separated hemispheres (Gazziniga)**	**Left hemisphere stroke (Jill-Bolte Taylor)**	**Autism (Williams and various sources (Caldwell))**
Brain chatter Inner speech	The 'interpreter' integrates data received from numerous systems in brain. Defines sense of self. Located in left hemisphere.	Received data incomplete, interpreter makes up stories to cover facts as they appear to present.	'Story teller'/ interpreter silenced. Dumps emotional baggage.	Incomplete, unfiltered and competing data presented to interpreter/ story teller. Lack of coherent story (looking for the pattern of what is happening interpreted) as danger, triggers self-defence system.
Sense of Self	Intact	Self-awareness intact – Joe says he just has a 'back-up brain'.	Intact until she loses consciousness.	Complaints of loss of sense of self, not just what but who I am. Adopting different personalities/ voices. Looks for self in mirror.
Boundaries	Defined (meditation)	Defined	Boundaries dissolve. Feels oceanic, inclusive, calm, peaceful.	Boundaries dissolve. Frightening. Seeking proprioceptive alternatives.
Language	Normal	Broca's area (left hemisphere) damaged. Unable to describe objects placed in right-hand field of vision.	Broca's and Wernicke's areas damaged. No receptive or executive speech.	Degree of damage to Broca's and Wernicke's areas varies from mild to extreme (no ability to decode incoming information or use speech). Speech facilitated in some individuals when stress level is reduced, suggesting problem is with anxiety/sensory overload.
Hypersensitivities	Within normal range.		Vision (glare). Sound (roar of shower water).	Sensitivity to external and internal (e.g. embarrassment) stimuli. Triggers sensory overload/autonomic storm.

As Jill's left hemisphere grinds to a halt, she manages with a heroic effort of will to phone a colleague for help but her words come out as unintelligible sounds, 'Waa, waa, waa' (failure in Broca's area, speech production). But her colleague's response also comes over in 'Waa –waa' (Wernicke's area – speech decoding). As Donna says, 'it's all just sounds'.

Comparing Jill's stroke failure to being able to interpret or produce speech, it would appear to be because the Broca's and Wernicke's areas have closed down. Donna's situation is different. Although she has the ability to speak four languages, she describes it as always an effort, since her ability to process and utilise speech is drowned out by unfiltered brain clutter, what she calls 'garbage'. It's like comparing a situation of involuntary surrender (Jill), with siege (Donna).

Not only is the autistic brain suffering from high levels of anxiety and stress but also neurological deficits mean that the processing necessary for effective action is severely disrupted and may be impossible. Are there any methods in generalised therapeutic terms that we can use to bypass the blockages? The guiding principle has to be that the brain is presented with signals that are easy to recognise, in a form that it can process. We already have a number of clues, especially the process of external cueing.

Chapter 8: Finding ways round the block

The blocks between receiving a stimulus and acting on it can occur in any number of different places. So far we have caught up with two. The Purkinje cell deficit may be responsible for some of the confusion between visual and auditory signals while they are being transmitted from the eye and ear to the region in the brain where they are processed. Donna Williams and others tell us that when they are wearing tinted lenses (cutting down on the confusion triggered by visual hypersensitivity) they can hear more clearly. It would be reasonable to suppose that, since they are not needed to transport scrambled visual signals, there are more Purkinje cells available to pick up the auditory signals.

The second deficit we have discussed in some detail is damage to the corpus callosum. Going back to Gazzaniga's work with Joe, we have seen how Joe's brain (in which the two halves had been surgically divided), was able to get round the lack of connection between his right brain and his left brain 'interpreter', by feeding into external clues which bypassed the gap.

Sometimes the compulsion to circumnavigate the block is so powerful that the brain devises its own (apparently independent) strategies. When Pranve wanted to return from the hall to the sitting room but was unable to make the transition, he threw his ball of string over the threshold, so now he had to come in, in order to retrieve it.

In her film *Jam-Jar*, Donna Williams provides a striking example of how she dealt with the chaos in her brain. First she describes the turmoil (slightly abbreviated).

'If you ask me, Donna, did you have lot of things back behind your conscious awareness that were overwhelming and you couldn't reason with them, put them all together and you couldn't put them all together and see the whole picture, I would say, yes. I was totally caught up in every moment. I never got the whole picture of me, who I was today, who I am going to be tomorrow or even a whole day or who anyone was in relation to anybody else – and so that is a huge turmoil inside of a person. You've got to find a way of putting it all together, otherwise you keep trying to run away from the turmoil.'

She goes on to describe how one day she simply got a typewriter, stuck a page in, and it all started to pour out.

'I was just sitting there with my fingers going and I was reading whatever was coming out at me and that it's telling me what is in me, so it wasn't really that I was talking to the pages of my book but that my pages of my book from here out here back through my eyes, talked to me and I listened, very big. So it's kind of like learning about life through writing my life out. This was the textbook that came from my own life. I read it and said, Oh my God, I'm going to take care of myself now. Now that I own it, now that it's in my hands, I know how I feel. I'm never going to let it get out of control again.'

The essence of this is that whereas before Donna could see what she had written about herself, she felt she was drowning in inaccessible fragments of stimuli; now it is 'out here', she has access to how she feels. In effect she is using an external cueing system (vision) to link feeling with conscious awareness.

The left brain does not know what the right brain is doing. Like Donna, Chris also tells me that very often she does not know what she is writing until she sees it on the page. And her brain uses external cueing to get round blockages using a different route:

'Reading to myself, the words go in but I forget them straight away. I can remember them if I mouth them (proprioceptive feedback) or read out loud (auditory feedback).'

Her brain has also devised a strategy for framing her thoughts so they are not drowned under sensory fragments. When I comment that some of her prose is actually written as poetry, she replies that sometimes she even thinks in verse.

'My head hurts, my chest is tight,
don't even know if I will last the night.
All these layers of life mean little to me,
cars and school and what's for tea?

Who am I? My light is under a bush.
All the needs of people, just had enough
crammed in my head from morning to night,
my brain giving up with little or no fight,
fragmented, demented, ready for a spree,
I'm trapped here inside, longing to be free,
free of torment, the tremors of pain,
the concepts repeated again and again.
Lost on me, into the chasm they fall
and I on my arse again relearn to crawl.'

Raw, undigested, but rhythm and rhyme, patterns and prosody drive her on, offer her a causeway she can cross to gain access to her emotions. (Many poets would agree that the urge to write is impelled by the desire to explore what we feel.)

Sometimes words do come more easily if they are floated on the rhythm of a tune. A number of parents say that their children can sing the words of a tune but are unable to speak. I have held my breath while in the company of people with whom I am working as they struggle to speak. Recalling Pranve (who had no speech apart from an occasional, 'Where's Charlene?' (his sister)), after we interact through his body language for three hours and he is really relaxed, it becomes absolutely clear that he is trying to articulate. His head moves up and down, round and round and his chin wobbles with effort of muscular synchronisation, a physical re-enactment of the phrase, 'getting your head round something'. After a number of fumbling attempts he manages the tune – and is able to produce the rhythm some time before he finally manages to sing the words – in this case, 'Baa-Baa Black Sheep'[98]. The delay between knowing what he wants to say and its execution is clearly due to an inability to organise the muscular movements necessary to facilitate articulation of the words that are evident to him in his brain, a complex process involving a number of different operations. For those of us not on the spectrum, for whom speech flows virtually simultaneously with the thought that triggers it, it is difficult to understand the struggles involved in its production.

1. Pranve has to know what he wants to say.

2. He has to place his muscles in the right positions.

3. His muscular movements have to be coordinated with correct breathing and use of vocal cords.

4. Finally Pranve has to combine all the different movements in the right order. Initially he is only capable of realising his intention through a few faltering but correct notes. Once he has got the mechanics right he bursts confidently into the first two lines, words and tune together.

This is a gross simplification and there are plenty of opportunities for failure.

The Stackhouse Wells model[99] identifies eleven different stages involving discrimination, representation and motor programming in the processing of one word, let alone the production of a sentence.

---

98   Caldwell P & Horwood J (2007) *From Isolation to Intimacy*. London: Jessica Kingsley Publishers.
99   Stackhouse Wells Model (1997) Cambridge Community Services NHS.

So it is a great achievement for him when Sam, who is unable to speak, tries to say my name. First, he manages 'Ah-ah' (the pitch and rhythm of, 'Phoe-be') and eventually manages 'Phoe', although he cannot get as far as articulating both syllables[100]. Although it is clear he would like to, he is defeated by his inability to synchronise and organise more than one syllable. Overloaded, he resorts to, 'Away' ('go away'), a word he has mastered when demand exceeds his capacity to articulate. The effort has overloaded him and he goes into spasmodic movements of his arms.

On this subject, a child with dyslexia tells her teacher that she needs a machine to organise and control her hands so that they can write down the words that she can see in her head[101]. It is not so much a cognitive deficit that is the problem as an ability to execute the correct muscular movements in the right order.

Summing up, our brains are ingenious and flexible and even where the corpus callosum is damaged, they may be able to develop ways of finding alternative routes. But what of those who are unable to bypass the impediment they encounter, where the left and right halves of the brain are totally separated and there are no ways round the block? Joe, whose brain is otherwise wired up normally, manages by using external cueing. Can this be applied to those who are unable to make any sort of connection (inside or outside) between the two halves of the brain?

The behavioural consequence of such drastic separation is that, although the right brain knows what the person wants to do, they do not have access to the left brain, so cannot place their desire in context, make up a coherent story and understand if we are unable to fulfil their wishes. Instead, they are instantly overloaded and thrown into an autonomic storm with all its disastrous sensations and pain. They are inflexible, all they perceive is the feeling of what they desire: they cannot understand that there may be reasons as to why they cannot have it.

Maree wants to go the shop. It is no good telling her that the shop is shut on a Sunday. She cannot make the connection between her desire and reason. The only possibility is to take her and show her that the shop door will not open: to physically place her hand on the door and so she can feel the door is locked. There is no other way of telling her since reasoning is not available to her. The link cannot be made.

On a personal note, the other day I was reminded how we may all need hints from another mode to prod us into action. If we want to remember something we build up a template, a composite sensory image with a number of different aspects;

---

100 Caldwell P (2010) *Autism and Intensive Interaction: Using body language to reach children on the autistic spectrum*. Film, Jessica Kingsley Publishers.

101 Personal communication.

a diversity that is useful as the brain begins to age and begins to encounter blockages on the way to accessing names.

Three weeks ago I struggled to recall the name of a strip of moorland.
I could see it in my mind and remembered that the name began with M but that was as far as it got – until I drove past a few days ago and, although I could not se the moor itself, I saw the path leading up to it. Immediately I knew it was Marston Moor. It was not that the memory of the word was lost but access to the name was denied, until I found an alternative route (in this case a visual lead in). The gestalt may be more than its constituents, but nevertheless a sufficient prod from one or more features can be enough to set in motion the process of recognition and recall.

Chapter 9: What am I doing?

I want to return now to an idea I have visited before[102], that is the loss of sense of self complained of by so many adults on the spectrum – a neglected aspect of the autistic experience. I am addressing this partly because it causes considerable emotional pain and undermines the quality of life in so many ways – and partly because there is additional information involving the nature of proprioception – and how this ties in with our perception of our self as an entity. If my approach seems roundabout and at times slightly laboured, this is because the subject matter is immensely complex. But it is an exploration that I hope will lead to a better understanding of what the autistic person means when they say that they have lost their sense of self.

Before we start, I do need to recap on proprioception, since it is a term on which the argument hinges but is one with which not every reader will be familiar. Proprioceptive messages are the messages that are transmitted to the brain from the different joints, tendons and muscles in our body. They tell us what we are doing.

When we think about proprioception, we need to distinguish between the stimulus we receive, the messages from the body to the brain, and our brain's ability to process these messages so that we become conscious of the original stimulus (and are able to respond to it).

But it is not simple, since our proprioceptive self-perception is also intimately linked with balance and boundaries and the incoming information from other senses such as vision. Disentangling these various lines is like trying to follow an individual bee as it goes about its work in a perceptual beehive. One needs to find ways of tagging the particular worker.

Firstly, I am going to start with myself since I know who I am better than I know who you are, at least I think I do. This is me. (Try following the same process in yourself.)

I know what I am doing, my senses tell me so. My eyes tell me what I see, my ears tell me what I hear, my nose, what I smell and several thousand sensors on my tongue (rapid turnover, each has a shelf-life of ten days), what I am tasting.

---

102 Caldwell P (2014) *The Anger Box*. Brighton: Pavilion Publishing and Media Ltd.

Together with muscles and joints in my body, they are all sending messages to my brain which translates for me the state of myself in relation to what is going on outside of me: they are working hand-in-hand informing me of my current sensory status. These will come into my brain in the form of electrical impulses and if all is well, will get picked up and processed by the relevant processing areas and converted into the images and soundscapes and sentient experience that make up my environment. They tell me about the world I am in and what I am doing in it.

But as Damasio points out, just as when my eyes see, or ears hear, my brain is not only given visual or auditory information but also reassurance that these receptive organs are in working order (or not).

So my perception of the world outside, in whatever form it arrives, is literally embodied in my physical self. This is important, so I repeat: I get my physical feeling of myself from other than my self[103]. At the same time, I not only learn what I am doing from this comprehensive package, but also learn where my boundaries are; what is 'me' and what is 'not me'. (Later we shall see that I not only get a sense of what I am but also the physical component of who I am – which will bring me to the verge of self-awareness.)

When it comes to how we are physically in contact with the outside world, our understanding is further complicated semantically since (in spite of the fact that a completely different set of sensors are involved), we use the word 'feeling' for both touch and pressure and emotional awareness. Touch is felt as the physical attributes of a surface, its texture, whether it is stationary or moving, hot or cold, etc. Pressure tells me about my internal state, what my joints and tendons and muscles are experiencing. And it is easy to confuse the two.

Here is Amber, a young woman with autism, talking about being undersensitive to touch when actually she is referring to hyposensitivity to proprioception – the sensors are different:

'I also experience under-sensitivity to some senses too but this mainly applies to my sense of touch. Due to my sense of touch being under-sensitive I can't really feel my surroundings very well. This sometimes bothers me as it makes me feel a bit detached and also makes it hard for me to ground myself when am anxious because, for example, when I'm sat down I can't really feel the chair behind me that much although I know it is there and I know I'm sat down. It can be hard living with sensory under-sensitivity because I often need to be given firm touch or hugs

---

103 Damasio A (2000) *The Feeling of What Happens: Body, emotion and the making of consciousness.* New York: Harcourt Brace & Company.

to help me feel grounded and this isn't always available. Saying this however, when I do get a hug it is one of the nicest feelings ever and makes me feel really comfortable and relaxed. It also helps me to feel grounded and can prevent me from going into meltdown or shutdown.' [104]

Practitioners need to differentiate between sensitivity to touch and pressure, because if a person is oversensitive to touch, being touched can be acutely painful, 'like a whole load of spiders crawling out of my skin'[105]. Touch can trigger a feeling of assault because the brain of the autistic person sends a message to their body warning it that it is being attacked and must defend itself. On the other hand Amber enjoys being hugged.

Back to myself, all in all I am being informed not just what I am doing and what it feels like – sitting on a squashy cushion on an office chair looking at my computer – but also receiving information about who I am in relation to who I am not: where I stop and where the outside world in the form of the chair and the screen starts. To further complicate the process, the sensory perceptions of touch and pressure combine with inputs from the balance system.

Just to take proprioception, when I am sitting down, not only do I feel pressure on my backside, feet, thighs and back telling me I am seated, but these messages conflate with information as to whether the chair is soft or hard and at what angle I am sitting, whether I am lounging or sitting bolt upright. When I stand up, I will get a completely different picture of my posture. Nevertheless, proprioception and balance together are in practice an almost secret positioning sense that records information but does not consciously bother me all the time with information telling me 'You are sitting down', 'You are standing up'. Not unless I make an effort to think about it. Unless I trip as I rise, I hardly notice what I am doing. But if I become unbalanced, I am suddenly presented with what is potentially a life-threatening event. Even then without thinking, I correct a 'whoops' situation with a reflex response.

So far, I have the feeling of the entity of my body, of body ownership, which is integrating what I am feeling. But it now appears that, deep in the middle of the brain, 'place cells' in the hippocampus are busy telling me where this feeling of my 'self' is located in regard to the environment[106]. So not only do I know where I am but also where my feeling of self is located; I know where 'I-am' is.

---

104 Amber's World. The Craven Gazette, April 2017.

105 Personal communication.

106 In 2014, the Nobel Prize was awarded to J O'Keefe, M-B Moser and El Moser for the discovery of 'place cells'.

I presume my feeling of my existence and my feeling of where 'I am' are in the same place, but again, this is not as simple as we should suppose, since under certain conditions our brains can be tricked into experiencing a reality shift, as our sense of self is re-located somewhere other than in our actual body.

So I want to look now at recent investigations which highlight this disconnection, and although this research does not start with autistic people, it may throw some light on what people on the spectrum mean when they say they are losing track of themselves; both 'who' and 'where' they feel they are.

This line of enquiry starts with schizophrenia (which although people on the spectrum may occasionally have schizophrenia, should not be confused with autism, which it sometimes is). As a young doctor, Henrik Ehrsson interviewed a man with schizophrenia who became completely 'switched off'. The accompanying nurse stood up and shook him hard, and he made connection again. She explained that when he shut down, he came to life again if he was shaken – that is vigorous proprioceptive input reconnected him. When Henrik asked his patient what he felt had happened, he described an 'out-of-body' experience, whereby he had left his body and was watching Henrik talk to this other man (himself) from outside[107].

Fascinated by the possibility of out-of-body experience, Henrik Ehrsson and his team have used advanced brain imaging technologies to follow what is going on in the brain during such experiences, and demonstrated that our brains can be fairly simply tricked into believing in the perceptual illusion of displacement 'of the sense of location of the feeling of self'.

In one study the subject sat square on to a small table with his right arm resting on the table. A screen set at right angles on the table blocked his view of his right arm. His left arm hung down by his left side, out of the picture. Directly in front of him what he can see is empty table surface. He looked fixedly at this. On the far side of the table, the experimenter stroked both his right (real) hand and the left hand (empty space) synchronously with a small paint brush. So initially, the subject feels, but doesn't see, the stroke on his right hand, while seeing but not (initially) feeling the stroke on the left, empty space[108]. In similar experiments, the left empty space is replaced by a rubber hand. Again, the subject can initially feel the stroke on their right hand but not see it, and can see, but not initially feel the stroke on the left rubber hand[109].

---

107 Ehrsson HH (2016) *What If We Could Leave Our Body and Have a New One?* TED Talk. Available at: https://www.youtube.com/watch?v=ZEhXX47PRvw (accessed September 2017).

108 Guterstam A, Biornsdotter M, Gentile G & Ehrsson HH (2015) Posterior cingulate cortex integrates the senses of self-location and body ownership. *Current Biology* **25** (11) 1416–1425.

109 Botnik M & Cohen J (1998) Rubber hands 'feel' touch that eyes see. *Nature* **391** (6669) 756.

Either way, awareness of the feeling of being stroked is lost in the right (real) hand (the one that is being stroked), instead the sensation of being stroked is felt in the area of the paint brush which is stroking the left empty space (where there is no actual hand), or, in experiments using a left artificial hand, in the rubber hand. That this is not just the result of a fertile imagination is demonstrated when the imaginary hand responds to a simulated attack with a hammer or knife in the same way as the actual hand. The sense of 'being a hand' has been transferred to empty space (or the rubber hand). It is suggested that 'the illusions spurious reconciliation of visual and tactile inputs relies upon a distortion of position sense'[110].

It is also possible to create total 'out-of body' illusions using head-mounted display screens and cameras, where the test person experiences themselves sitting two meters behind themselves.

'You are looking at yourself – you know it is you but it doesn't feel like you any more, it feels like another person... you know it can't be happening but it feels real.' (Participant in research)

The experiments have grown more sophisticated with the use of MRI scanners. It is now possible to follow which parts of the brain are being activated during an out of body experience. While the brain is receiving visual and proprioceptive signals and passing them on to the sensory integration centres, the place cells in the hippocampus are locating the sense of feeling of self in a particular environmental context, telling the brain where it is feeling itself – a kind of internal GPS. Ehrsson sums up:

'Owning a body, and that of being localised somewhere in space, are two key components of human consciousness that are triggered by activity in different parts of the brain, which talk to each – are integrated – through the posterior cingulate cortex.' [111]

One system integrates sensory intake (giving the sensation of myself), and the second, differentiates myself from other than myself and tells me where I am in space. Critically, if these two systems are working in synchrony, my feeling of self is experienced as in-body – but if for some reason they are out of sync, such as tiredness or illness, the GPS can give a faulty reading, with the illusion of out-of-body experience. This may involve not just a part of the body being displaced, but that of the whole body being outside itself, inside some other 'false' person and looking back at the real body-self.

---

110 Botnik M & Cohen J (1998) Rubber hands 'feel' touch that eyes see. *Nature* **391** (6669) 756.

111 Guterstam A, Biornsdotter M, Gentile G & Ehrsson HH (2015) Posterior cingulate cortex integrates the senses of self-location and body ownership. *Current Biology* **25**(11) 1416–1425.

This is where we come back to autism and the overall problems of disconnection between different areas of the brain. In the normal sequence of events those of us not on the spectrum differentiate between in-body and out-body experience of where our feeling of 'self' is, that we have a sense of boundary between self and other. To put it personally, I know where I stop and you start.

But for Chris, who has a diagnosis of Aspergers syndrome, she may lose this sense of her self as a separate entity:

'I find myself being fragments of other people ... I don't know which bits are me; who I am – and who everyone else is, is not clear – the edges between us seem to soften, sometimes they include everyone else rather than just me, I can't be separate ... I can't see all of myself at the same time. Until I look in the mirror (or, in her case, lights up a cigarette – a physical sensation that 'brings everything back')*, I have no idea what I look like, who I am.'* [112]

If one compares the out-of-body experience of Henrik Ehrsson's patient with that of Chris, what brings them both back to awareness of self is switching their brain to an alternative processing route, one that allows the brain to reconnect; physical shaking in the case of Ehrsson's patient, and for Chris, the sensation of inhaling smoke or visual recognition by looking in the mirror and seeing herself contained within a frame.

Similarly in an evaluation of his repetitive behaviors, Tito Mukhopadhyay[113] says:

'I am calming myself. My senses are so disconnected, I lose my body. So I flap (my hands). If I don't do this, I feel scattered and anxious ... I hardly realized I had a body ... I needed constant movement, which made me get the feeling of my body ... I need to move constantly to be aware that I am alive and my name is Tito.'

Chris and Tito share with Donna Williams a feeling of disembodiment. Like Jill Bolte-Taylor describing the affects of her left-brain stroke, they have lost their sense of being a separate being. But in this respect it is interesting that both say that, as a consequence, they not only have problems with the 'what' they are, that is their physical self-image, but also with their psychological image, the 'who' they are. This is a problem we shall come back to later.

In the same way that Tito needs to flap his hands to restore his self image, Richard uses kinaesthetic anchorage to correct his feeling of non-attachment, physically putting pressure on his body to tell it where it is and what it is doing:

---

112 Caldwell P (2014) *The Anger Box*. Brighton: Pavilion Publishers and Media Ltd.
113 Tito Mukhopadhyay, transcript of excerpt from CBS *60 Minutes* segment.

'I have a poor sense of my body and where it is. My bicycle provides a framework to fit my body with five contact points, I feel connected on a bicycle, there is a lovely warm comfortable sense I am an embodied being. I get messages from my body, I don't feel like I am floating somewhere nearby watching my body from a distance. It's good to feel like a flesh and blood human being... and know where I am and what size I am.' [114]

In some ways the bicycle becomes iconic: as a speaker, it is enough for Richard to hold the bicycle rather than physically having to mount it. Just knowing it is there is enough to centre him.

One solution to this feeling of lack of boundaries is to wear a pressure vest such as the 'Squease vest'. Defined as a personal hug, the Squease vest is a gilet that can be worn underneath a shirt and inflated to provide an artificial boundary. Richard explains: 'the body feels contained, it doesn't feel as if other people are going to invade you'[115] and as a young man named Joseph describes, 'the body no longer feels as if it is blowing itself apart'[116].

So far we have looked at the difficulties arising if the sensory integration system and the place cell 'GPS' are not synchronised. While one might suppose that this is due to lack of physical connections between systems, the whole problem is compounded by the levels of anxiety which interfere with the integration of proprioceptive signals.

Listen to Donna Williams, who has taught us so much about the affective world of her autism. She describes the experience of having no well defined boundary between self and the rest of the world in extremely negative terms, she is so afraid she comes to a halt; 'If you have trouble processing information or retrieving it in a connected way you can become disconnected physically, like being disembodied'[117].

The relationship between proprioception and anxiety is extremely well demonstrated in a clip from a BBC documentary about dissection of the foot[118]. George McGavin (not on the spectrum) has no problems when he is asked to walk along a narrow plank on the floor. Suitably harnessed and required to walk the

---

114 McGuire R (2014) *I Dream in Autism*. CreateSpace Independent Publishing Platform.

115 Personal communication.

116 Personal communication.

117 Williams D (2014) *Autism: An inside-out approach*. London: Jessica Kingsley Publishers.

118 Clip from 'Fear of Falling' from BBC4 film 'The incredible human foot' (fast forward to the 50 minute mark if you don't want to watch the foot dissection). Brilliant description of the relationship between anxiety and proprioception: http://www.bbc.co.uk/iplayer/episode/p01mv2rj/dissected-2-the-incredible-human-foot

same plank when it is suspended six foot up in the air, he hesitates and then comes to a halt, although he was perfectly capable of traversing the same plank when it was on the ground. He is paralysed by anxiety which interferes with the proprioceptive messages to his brain telling him what he is doing. He becomes locked into a cycle of distraction, a psychological anxiety that produces a real physical response and he comes to a halt. The plank is the same width but he simply cannot move forward. What is happening is that his 'awareness of danger' anxiety messages to the brain are interfering and overriding his proprioceptive and balance messages.

One of the most characteristic features of autism is anxiety, triggered by an amygdala that is set on red alert. When repetitive behaviours no longer hold the sensory overload at bay, the autistic brain triggers the body's self-defence system in one of three ways: flight, aggression (to self or others), or rather less commonly, simply closing down, known as 'shutdown'.

In their seminal paper on shutdown, Loos and Loos Millar[119] observed a child who, when over-stimulated, became limp and would fall into deep sleep from which, although conscious, she could not be roused. (This differed from conscious avoidance; once set on this path it was not possible to divert her using her favourite toy.) The authors associated this behaviour with over-arousal of the basolateral amygdala (BLA) and release of the stress mediating neurotransmitter, corticotrophin releasing factor (CRF).

Individual accounts suggest that, in its struggles to avoid sensory overload, an autistic person's brain may adopt more than one strategy. Two authors give inside-out accounts of what this feels like. The first is Amber describing alternatives, an either/or process:

'Meltdowns and shutdowns happen when everything has become too much and stress gets on top of you. Both meltdowns and shutdowns are caused by too much stress or being overwhelmed and overloaded but they present themselves differently. Meltdowns happen when you become overwhelmed by a situation and can cause you to lose control of your behavior. This can be in verbal form (such as shouting, screaming or crying) or physical form (such as lashing out or presenting with challenging behavior). For me when I am going to meltdown it feels like everything is building up inside and feels like I'm going to explode and I try and control it for as long as I can but sometimes it builds up too much and spills out and this is when I have a meltdown. Shutdowns are when things become too much but present themselves to me by being unable to function or move and it feels like

---

119 Loos GH & Loos Miller IM (2004) *Shutdown States and Stress Instability in Autism.* Cuewave Corporation.

you can't speak or do anything. When I am going into shutdown I slowly withdraw further and further in my mind from my surroundings until I no longer feel like I can interact or respond to people. Both meltdowns and shutdowns are often caused by either sensory overload (when your senses become too over-stimulated) or social overload (being exposed to too much social interaction).'[120]

The second account is sequential:

'My most recent shutdown started as a meltdown. My brain was going through all its usual short-circuits when some synaptic gap gets crossed. Or something. One minute I was out of control, smacking myself on the face, as one does, and the next minute I was on the floor, unable to move. I started to get tunnel vision. My hearing began to get fuzzy. My vision closed off like turning off an old tube-driven television, closing down to a tiny dot of light and winked out just as my hearing entirely cut out, leaving me alone in the numbly terrifying darkness.'[121]

Shutdown is not always dramatic. A man looking at a book, is arrested in the middle of trying to turn over the page. No matter how he is encouraged to proceed he cannot move on. Asked later, he says, 'I needed time to think'. One interpretation of this is that he needs time to organise his muscles in order to get them in the correct sequence to move on. It does not help to talk to someone who is going into shutdown as it adds to the overload, but sometimes external cueing and gesture will get them going again. A child who cannot move from her class to the hall is enabled to proceed by giving her a heavy chair to carry which she will use to sit on when she reaches the hall.

I should like to suggest it is possible that people on the spectrum are not so much low on proprioceptive messages (hyposensitive to proprioception), but that these pressure messages are reaching the brain but when they get there they are overwhelmed by anxiety messages (anxiety rooted in the unpredictability of their sensory perception. As Therese Jolliffe says, 'I live in terror all the time'[122], terror that something terrible will happen – for example that sensory overload will tip her into an autonomic storm with its painful and frightening consequences).

A correspondent speaks of 'unconscious proprioception', a description that puzzles me, since proprioception is felt, so how can it be unconscious? But consideration suggests that I am confusing the proprioceptive message from the body to the brain with 'becoming aware of the message'. Going back to George McGavin's failure to be able to walk the plank when it was suspended in the air, perhaps

---

120 Amber's World. The Craven Gazette, April 2017.

121 Personal Communication.

122 Jolliffe T, Lansdown R & Robinson C (1992) Autism: a personal account. *Communication* **26** 3 (hard copies available from the NAS).

messages (such as those which maintain homeostasis) are being sent but are getting drowned out by anxiety. And these unacknowledged, unrecognised messages are adding to sensory overload.

In an attempt to re-establish a sense of boundaries and connection with their in-body self, many children run around desperately trying to give themselves self-stimulus that has meaning; banging themselves, rocking, jumping, climbing and scratching and biting, anything that will tell themselves what they are doing and where their boundaries are. It is not that they are not getting the messages, so much as that fear is overriding the capacity of brain to process and integrate them.

Depending on how much this low sense of proprioception has an impact on their lives, children who are undersensitive to proprioception and have a poor sense of boundary may feel secure enough indoors, where the walls of the room form a boundary that has meaning – but outside is an endless space in which they are completely lost. They don't know where they are or what they are doing. They may refuse to go outside; their body feels as if it will explode or disintegrate, there is nothing to hold it together.

Some people on the spectrum manage to work out ways of giving themselves artificial boundaries. A young woman wears a loose jacket indoors but needs a tight coat she can feel when outside. A child who is quiet in class becomes desperate in the playground. He walks around compulsively beating the boundaries of his playground with a plastic hoop during break time, giving himself physical feedback about the limits of space. He stops and relaxes when he spots his image in my camera lens. When his image is framed he is able to check visually on his low proprioceptive perception of his self.

A woman, who has autism and severe learning disabilities, sits on the floor all the time, where she can feel herself on a secure base. She will not go out at all, hanging onto the door frame and bellowing, that is until I manage to make it clear to her that although she and I are going out (I used gesture), we are coming back here to where she feels contained (again, I use gesture and point to the floor where she is sitting). She is affectively paralysed by fear. Once I have let her know (in a way that has meaning for her) that she is coming back to somewhere that is familiar, her anxiety is reduced and she recovers her ability to move. She is now able to mobilise her muscles and we go out for a walk together.

Chapter 10: Evolutionary interlude

Having got this far, I have a rather surprising confession to make; one that I include because it illustrates how widely the brain can cast its net when it comes to the sources of our ideas, and how being receptive to metaphor can lead the brain to see things in a different light.

I would have been unable to write much of the latter part of this book if it had not been for a chance meeting with a large maybug staggering across the lane, clearly on its last (six) legs. This insect encounter led to a train of thought about how it feels to be an insect, and in particular what would be the consequences of walking round in a suit of armour for defence and support, an exoskeleton with well defined boundaries, instead of depending on a rod up one's back, an endoskeleton supporting soft boundaries. This led on to thinking about proprioception in general and what it is that defines our boundaries, sense of self, consciousness, self-awareness and even, intrigued by a paper that had the title 'Do fruit flies have emotions?', to consider the limits we all place on emotional experience. And also, how do people with autism experience emotions? Do they always experience feelings in the same way as those of us not on the spectrum?

Clearly this is a mammoth task and I shall try and stick to aspects that affect autism, either directly or indirectly. But first of all I want to look at what we mean by sensory awareness, both in the sense of sensory stimulus received from outside the body, and also awareness that we have of what is going on inside our bodies (sentience). Rather than diving into complex philosophical arguments on the nature of what we call self – and hoping to find some glimmer of what it feels like to be something other than ourselves, I am coming back to my maybug.

My reason for pursuing this somewhat unconventional route is that the combination of insect brain structure with their behavioural responses may throw some light on our human evolution of consciousness. But first of all, a warning for those who are not familiar with the evolutionary tree: in no way are we descended from insects, we evolved in parallel.

So how does the insect brain differ from that of humans and what might this tell us about the origins (and presence) of consciousness? And anyway, what do we mean by consciousness? As far as we are concerned we drift through most of our existence.

In their fascinating book *The Ancient Origins of Consciousness*, Feinberg and Mallatt summarise the evolution of consciousness[123]. They distinguish between three different levels of awareness. The primary and most basic level of awareness concerns reception of stimuli from the external environment, as perceived by vision, smell, hearing, taste and touch receptors. Responses to these which are localised, having little or no intrinsic 'goodness' or 'badness' ('this is "OK" for me or "Not OK" for me'). At this level, images do not normally impinge on conscious thought, unless passed on to higher levels of processing. He makes the distinction between this reflexive sensory consciousness to the external environment (knowing what is going on round one) and sentient consciousness (the capacity for internal feelings and affects)[124].

The second level of consciousness may be thought of as a half-way house, between extroceptive perception (perception of stimuli originating from outside) and internal perception of emotions. Stimuli refer both to the inner body and external environment. They may be experienced both as local mental images and as inner visceral and affective states.

And the third level of consciousness is affective, one in which we experience affect and become aware that we are experiencing emotions. As we shall see, as well as physical awareness of our surroundings, our emotions contribute to our feeling of our self.

Feinberg and Mallatt go on to discuss a number of criteria for the evolution and achievement of consciousness, including the possession of a variety of distance senses with a high level of resolution (for example, large compound eyes in insects), and the presence of structures with functionally the same form and structure as in the human brain.

But in order to avoid the dangers of anthropomorphism, we cannot just infer the level of an insect's level of perception from its behavioural responses; we need to look and see if it has the necessary brain parts to feel in the affective sense.

One of its more interesting aspects is that of the gap between the brain firing and the sensory experience; that is, an experience is always referred from the brain to either out in the world or, in the case of pain or emotion, somewhere (other than in the brain) in the body[125].

To be conscious, in the sense of self-aware, insects would have to share our capacity to form visual and other sensory maps in the back of the brain that

---

123 Feinberg TE & Mallatt M (2016) *The Ancient Origins of Consciousness*. Cambridge, MA: MIT Press.
124 *Ibid.*
125 *Ibid.*

correspond to what they see. They must also be able to merge the sensory inputs from different senses. Finally, there have to be localised areas for memory (so called 'mushroom bodies' because of their shape in insects) and mechanisms for selective attention that have been demonstrated in bees, fruit flies and scarabs.

Processing becomes more complicated as the forebrain evolves; messages are passed backwards and forwards around an intricate web of checks and balances. From the point of view of autism, our capacity for consciousness is not only dependent on which processing systems are present but also, even if they are present, whether or not they are effectively connected – and if they are, whether they are sending messages to the correct destination for processing a particular input.

Taken as a whole, while insects score surprisingly highly on the scale of sensory perception, showing fear responses, drinking more alcohol if sexually frustrated and having an elaborate 'internal sat-nav' using the stars for orientation, the question that Feinberg asks is why, given their extraordinary capacity for diversification, did they never develop the large wrap-round cerebral cortex that allows humans to feel self-awareness. His suggestion is that as the insect grows and enlargement has to be accommodated by shedding its hard covering, the necessary increase in brain/body size would have led to increased vulnerability to predators.[126]

Returning to the maybug in his suit of armour, I should like to suggest a possible alternative to the failure of insects to develop the cerebral cortex which would permit self-awareness; one that links the capacity of the human brain for self-awareness to our need for proprioceptive confirmation. What insects have and we humans lack, is a portable boundary, a resource that defines itself by instant feedback. (One may get some idea of this instant feedback when wearing a wet-suit out of water. Similarly, an autistic person who is low on proprioception and hence a sense of boundaries may find relief in wearing a tight pressure jacket.) In proprioceptive terms, during his evolution, the maybug and his arthropod relations had little need to reach out to explore and interpret the physical sensations of the world outside himself: a hard outer boundary, the tegument, or what one might call the rind, provided on-tap, instant proprioceptive definition and feedback. Or to put it another way, it is not so much that insects failed to evolve a large cerebral cortex but that in our search for proprioceptive confirmation, we soft-boundaried humans were forced to develop one.

---

126 Feinberg E & Mallatt JM (2016) *The Ancient Origins of Consciousness*. Massachusetts: The MIT Press.

Perhaps it is only we who have soft boundaries, who have had to develop a more complex brain that allowed us to reach out in order to confirm ourselves and become self-aware in relation to our surroundings. Maybe it is our impressible flesh instead of a tegument wall that leads us to physically explore the world outside ourselves. Perhaps this search for confirmation is where our curiosity comes from.

Chapter 11: I 'selfie', therefore I am

I am grateful to this irreverent slant on Descartes' famous axiom[127] as it very accurately pinpoints the modern dilemma of existential loneliness and the quest for confirmation. I need to be 'liked' a thousand times over. But no matter how urgent my desire, I am never satisfied. Why not? What is this sense of self, the self that I know that I am, that is so wobbly and yet so fundamental to my psychological well-being?

Humans are not naturally hermits and most of us acknowledge the need to be part of the herd for protection. If we don't have a strong enough sense of self we are vulnerable to feelings of rejection which, from a biological point of view, can be life-threatening. One of the more unpleasant circumstances is to be 'sent to Coventry'. Cast out from the community, we become commodities, objects, of no mutual account. In a flock of geese, the normal coupling is one gander to two geese. If there are not enough geese to go round, the surplus gander separates himself, goes off, stops eating and dies.

There are scientists and philosophers who believe that the whole idea of 'self' is an illusion, that it has no real substance but is rather a sense of 'this person that is me' emerging from the sum of brain activity; a compartmentalised brain where the different bits can talk to each other, reflecting inwards to produce an illusion of individuality: a grand total of nature and experience that produces the feeling of me being who I am (including and accepting the bits I would rather not be)[128].

But from the practical point of view of knowing ourselves as a discrete entity, whether or not our self-awareness is an illusion hardly matters; if we lack it we are vulnerable, in the sense that we feel unattached. Without a centre from which to reach out, we are unable to differentiate ourselves.

This sense of self is precious: to gaze directly at the 'I' we call our inner self, quivering, naked, the I that is our essence, is to be aware of a state of being that is our quidity (the essense of our being).

---

127 Walker H (2017) *I selfie therefore I am*. The Times **12 March**.

128 Hood B (2012) *The Self Illusion: How the social brain creates identity*. Oxford: Oxford University Press.

It is self-awareness that lifts the corner of the curtain onto 'I am'. Human beings may well be the only animals that are aware they are aware. 'Even then, we are mostly just conscious in the minimal sense, rarely pausing for self-reflection'[129].

Different from our awareness of our sensory needs, or even of reflection on our affective states, 'I am' is the dynamic statement of our existence rather than simply any old agent of responsiveness. Afraid to look, we guard it closely, even from ourselves. This is the 'I' that both speaks and is uttered.

Are we more than just our wiring? Is this what human beings have learned to call the soul? Nevertheless, on the ground, we do need something concrete to hold onto, since it is easier to come to terms with an image than with an abstraction. How can I bear to look at the sky and admit that what I see goes on forever, when it is more comfortable to imagine it as the upturned lid of a soup tureen, something close and to hand?

It is precisely this sense of identity that defines our being. It is a place from which we can engage with the world. Without it we have no defences and no centre from which we can reach out. So in human terms, how do we build up awareness of our unique core of 'selfness'? Where do we begin?

Just as my sensory experience gives me a picture of my boundaries (the physical me and not-me of my world), so also my feelings build up an awareness of my psychological boundaries, the 'who' of who I am. While I not only feel stimuli that come from outside, and the visceral stimuli that originate internally, I can also reflect on what these sensations mean. The light is switched on: I am self-aware, and I can even reflect on my capacity for self-reflection.

The first inkling we have of a feeling of physical self in relation to the world beyond ourselves comes when we sense (and tune into) the rhythmic pressure of our mother's heart beat through the amniotic fluid. This contact starts weeks before our hearing comes on line and we can hear the sound of its beat. But pressure and rhythm come first.

After our hazardous passage through the birth canal, we arrive in this world primed for interaction. We have to try and make sense of the bombardment of bright lights, noises, movements and strangeness as quickly as possible. So we latch on very quickly to anything that does make sense to our immature perception.

---

129 Feinberg TE & Mallatt M (2016) *The Ancient Origins of Consciousness: How the brain created experience*. Cambridge, MA: MIT Press.

In the following paragraphs I shall use the term 'mother', or 'adult', to cover the adult participant in the interactions but this should not be taken to exclude paternal involvement; it simply reflects the traditional role of mothers as the most likely to be closely involved in intimate interaction.

Until recently research has focused on the infant's ability to copy the mother's initiatives, suggesting that even a twenty minute old infant will copy her mother when her mother sticks out her tongue, tentatively at first and then with increasing confidence, as he or she learns that if they make certain muscular movements or sounds, they will get a recognisable and specific response. However, more recent investigations suggest that babies tend to stick out their tongues (or wriggle their fingers) anyway, if they see something that catches their attention[130]. What had been taken as the capacity to copy, was more likely simply an awareness response – 'there is something out there that is attracting my attention'. A considerable weight of cognitive developmental theory rests on the theory that that the skill of imitation does not emerge until the second year and is therefore emergent rather than innate.

Maybe we have been viewing this crucial developmental stage through the eyes of our own fascination with imitation and the ensuing dialogue that can evolve. Looked at from the baby's point of view; perhaps it is recognition rather than imitation that is critical, recognition in the sense of matching up what the infant sees and hears when it is copied, with a neural pathway it has already begun to map out.

So, from the baby's perspective, 'If I make a certain movement, and my mother copies it, I can feel it happen in myself when I make it but also see what my initiative looks like in the mirror of my mother's response'. So my infant brain is using my senses to probe the world, looking for recognisable answers to my actions, building up my sense of my, 'I know what I am doing'. (The responses to my infant initiatives do not have to be exact copies – but do have to be near enough for the underlying sound or movement or rhythm to be recognised and matched to the template which my infant brain already has.) Meanwhile, my mother is on the lookout for my new born initiatives. She is primed to welcome me into a world of meaning.

So if I, baby, make a sound or wave my hand, you, mother, are going to gurgle, or wave back to me. This tells my infant brain that the particular set of muscular movements I made, trigger this particular outcome. A new pathway of connections between nerves (synapses) is being established in my brain, a step towards my, 'I know what

---

130 Jones SS (2009) The development of imitation in infancy. Philosophical Transactions of the Royal Society B: *Biological Sciences* **364** (1528) 2325–2335.

I'm doing' map. Mother and I have established a way of talking to each other that has meaning for both of us. We are using a common language to communicate. My mother is responding with feedback that I recognise, confirming what I am doing.

In the face of the vast number of reports by parents (including my personal ones), of imitation by infants during their first year and the joy of reciprocal interaction (where the mother or mother figure initiates and the baby responds), the effect of this focus on imitation, has been to obscure the importance in development of the baby's capacity to recognise the maternal response to its initiatives and the confirmative affect this recognition permits.

Maybe it is the ability to recognise parental confirmation at this stage, rather than a capacity to mimic that is critical in development. This is illustrated particularly well in a recent interchange with an eight-month-old baby in my family.

Indy sat upright on the sofa and wobbled in a crack between two cushions. I picked up the rhythm of her movement and wobble up and down. She responded, tentatively at first, and then this developed into a mutual bouncing game. She waved her arms in delight. Our 'conversation' continued for at least ten minutes. Indy's 'bouncing' was a completely new trick, her parents confirmed that she had never done it before – but her initial accidental wobble gave her a template, so she is able to match my response to a motor pattern that is already in place. Since our initial encounter, she has widened her capacity to relate her bouncing to various 'like-enough' responses, such as 'dancing waving arms'. She is using her bouncing to respond. While it is her current, 'I like this' response, she is not only building her brain-map but also learning that it is fun to interact with the world outside herself – that there is a world out there which is user-friendly.

Drawing on descriptions by Papousek and Papousek[131], Daniel Stern describes the give and take nature of the exchanges between mother and baby:

'What is striking in these descriptions is that the mother is almost always working within the same modality as the infant. And in the leadings, followings, high-lightings and elaborations that make up her turn in the dialogue, she is generally performing close or loose imitations of the infant's behaviour. If the infant vocalises, the Mother vocalises back, similarly, if the infant makes a face, the Mother makes a face. However the dialogue does not remain a stereotypic boring sequence of repeats, back and forth, because the Mother is constantly introducing modifying imitations, providing a theme and variation format that slightly changes in her contribution at each dialogic turn.'

---

131 Stern D (1985) *The Interpersonal World of the Infant: A view from psychoanalysis and developmental psychology*. New York: Basic Books Inc.

Or to put it simply, baby initiates, mother confirms and baby and mother build on this exchange. It provides a platform from which to expand.

Damasio[132] highlights the importance of such recognition and confirmation in his observation that when we perceive a message from the world outside our selves, we get information not only about the source but, as importantly, or possibly more importantly, there is a second message to our brains which tells us that our receiving organ is in working order.

In this way, messages about our state of ourselves are physically embodied. We learn about ourselves and the boundaries between us and other through confirmation. It is confirmation that allows us to integrate incoming stimuli and 'move on'.

At this point I want to turn to the experiences of people who are on the autistic spectrum and for whom this system does not always work so smoothly. If the responses coming from the mother or mother figure are not getting through because their processing in the brain of the child is scrambled, they are not going to perceive the outside world as responding to their initiatives. They are going to find it difficult to receive the confirmation they need that would help them to move on, but just as essential, build a good internal map of their body – and hence sense of self.

So, an autistic person will be likely to have had problems during the differentiation of the nerves in the brain so that the physical messages they receive may be distorted. Children have said to me, 'My brain's not wired up properly'. While this seems harsh, it is a fairly accurate description of what can go wrong during development. The effect is that sounds and visual and physical sensations overlap. A person on the spectrum may not be able to filter out inessential stimuli and process incoming information fast enough, and the brain struggles all the time to build a coherent picture of what is happening. In addition, there may be parts of the brain where the nerve cells have too many, or too few connections – and the linkages between these areas may be missing. On top of this, the default system, which should be clearing out the rubbish, doesn't work. So it is not surprising that some will give up the struggle and retreat from the sensory overload into an inner world where there is less demand. They are conscious and aware, but turn their back on a world that threatens to overwhelm them, in order to survive.

Autistic people may do this by focusing on a particular sensation that has meaning for them. At its most basic, they develop a conversation between the brain and the body. So the brain might say to the body, 'scratch your hand'. The hand scratches and sends back a physical message (proprioceptive feedback) to

---

132 Damasio A (1999) *The Feeling of What Happens: Body and emotion in making of consciousness*. London: William Heinemann.

the brain saying, 'done it'. This brain-body conversation is self-confirming. The brain continues to get feedback that is meaningful and which tells them (in this case) about the boundary of their fingers.

To recap, in the middle of sensory chaos, in order to have at least one sensation whose outcome is predictable, people on the spectrum may focus on one sensation to the exclusion of other incoming sensory stimuli; a behaviour they call 'stimming', short for 'self-stimulation'. As Sean Barron says, 'When I do this I know what I am doing'[133]. It is hard-wired in and does not require elaborate brain processing.

When Damasio points out that we embody ourselves through our interactions with others, what if the messages that reach our brain are being hopelessly skewed (overwhelmed as we have seen in the case of proprioception by anxiety) so that we have to spend our whole lives trying to work out what is happening around us. And we are afraid because we are overheating our sympathetic nervous system which we are afraid will result in an autonomic storm. The only hope we have is to cut down on anxiety by focusing on a single activity to cut out the overwhelming and painful incoming stimuli, or to try and separate ourselves from the source of these stimuli by running away, freezing or showing aggression.

Joe spells out the relationship between his need for physical confirmation and his loss of sense of self[134]. As a young boy, he jumped up and down incessantly. He was taken to see a psychiatrist, who took a stern line with him. She told him that he had to stop jumping, that when he walked out of the door of her room, he was never to jump again. Being an obedient child he conformed to her direction, but says, 'at that moment, I lost my sense of self'. He needed the physical confirmation of impact to define his boundaries. Prevented from jumping, Joe lost the messages that defined not only his physical parameters but also his psychological centre.

Confirmation is central to our picture of ourselves. This is not just about infancy and not just about autism. We are constantly seeking to confirm this image throughout our lives. We touch our selves, rub our hands, wriggle our feet and twitch one way or another, or seek confirmation from the outside world. Each time we are reminding ourselves not only of the boundaries of that self but also of the existence of inner psychological self.

If we are unable to extract confirmation from the world outside, we may self-stimulate in some way or another – the degree of conscious control varies.

---

133 Barron J & Barron S (2002) *There's a Boy In There: Emerging from the bonds of autism*. Texas: Future Horizons.

134 Joe in *Being Autistic*. Published by Autscape, no longer in print.

I meet May at an autism conference. Since she knows she is going to be under sensory pressure, she has brought along a cotton reel with four pins in the top and a ball of wool. While she and I talk, her fingers are concentrating on 'french knitting' and the physical repetitive action of slipping sequential loops wool over each pin in turn, with a tube coming out of the lower end of the hole.) In order to maintain some control over her slippery environment she is focusing on a particular activity. All her physical attention is on the repetitive movement, but at the same time she is self-aware as she looks at me and we laugh together when she says it is 'socially acceptable stimming'. May knows exactly what she is doing but is also aware of the effect it offers to people around her. She is simultaneously conscious of herself and others.

At the risk of labouring the point (because it is central to my argument), we get a large part of confirmation of who we are and what we are doing through the experience of our boundaries and embodiment by sensing the world outside ourselves. We are constantly looking to top up this sensory stimulus, either by self-stimulus or by reaching out for more. And repeated confirmation, using one sense to check up on another, re-enforces neural pathways and our general picture we have of ourselves.

Turning now to the psychological sense of self, if a person is autistic their defensive reactions may mark them out as 'odd' in the eyes of the non-autistic world. The word they may hear most often is, 'No', since they are frequently being redirected away from the particular behaviour on which they are focusing to try and give themselves at least one point of stability. This will increase their anxiety, with behavioural consequences. Expression of how they feel is rejected; they are not even allowed to know that their feelings are real.

Self-awareness is a luxury for people with autism since, compounded by society's expectations that the autistic person will conform to its norms, the brain is desperately busy trying to sort out the confusion arising from hypo and hypersensitivities.

To return to ducks and geese: their behaviour towards weaker members of the respective flocks differs profoundly. Ducks reject and attack their 'disabled' offspring, while geese round them up and protect them. Unfortunately, we humans behave like ducks, in the sense that we instinctively reject behaviour which does not conform to the norm and try our best to steer it towards what we perceive as socially acceptable. In pursuing this line, we invalidate the people they feel themselves to be. The consequence is that since we either ignore or rebuff them, they lose confidence and contact with their feelings, and since the image of ourselves is shaped by our emotions, they lose their sense of self.

Just how much this matters is made very clear by Susan Ward Davis in her presentation to Autism Oxford[135].

Susan struggled all her life with feeling odd, different, but she was 62 before she received a diagnosis of autism. She had always thought there 'was something wrong with me ... and spent a lifetime trying to be invisible so that no-one would notice me. I always had low self-esteem, lacked confidence and felt inadequate'. Her difficulties with people triggered feelings of stress, anxiety and depression. She spent her childhood and teenage years masking her difficulties. And as a result of her efforts to fit in, she became a chameleon, is even now is, 'still unsure who is the real me ... Our coping skills come at a huge cost to our emotional well-being. All the time we are trying to be something we are not.'

She quotes Richard McGuire, talking in this case about people with learning disability:

'Because of the way learning disabled people receive therapy and perhaps been discouraged from behaving in ways that are natural to them, they are very often profoundly out of contact with who they are.'

But, whether or not they are learning disabled, or intellectually brilliant, the same is true for autistic people. 'We need to receive validation (confirmation), for who we are.'

Donna Williams says, 'I had created an ego that was detached from the self which was still shackled by crippled emotions... I could say what I thought but not what I felt'[136]. Like those of us not on the spectrum, people with autism come in all shapes and sizes. The question is how can those of us who get a well-defined sensory picture of our surroundings help those who are struggling to make sense of their world? Our attitude needs to be that of geese rather than ducks, the provision of a nurturing environment for their affective state which is meaningful for a particular individual rather than that of conditional behaviourism.

Bearing in mind the necessity for tranquility so the autistic brain is not being overburdened with sensory 'garbage' (a term used by Donna Williams to describe excess unfiltered sensory overload), as well as the notion that one size does not fit all, to encourage a healthy sense of self we need to adopt a holistic approach. This should involve:

---

135 Ward Davis S (2017) *Who am I? Validating the person.* Autism Oxford Presentation 22 February 2017.

136 Personal Communication.

1. Supportive strategies which reduce sensory overload and facilitate engagement, rather than behavioural training (which neglects sensory deficits and the anxiety and pain that can be triggered when they are steered away from their points of stability).

2. Modification of the environment to reduce stimuli that are difficult to process and increase anxiety.

3. Validation of how the person feels, especially their negative feelings.

Chapter 12: Feelings

The whole subject of feeling is confused by the way in which the word 'feeling' and emotion are used in the literature, since there is often little distinction between physically feeling a sensation and our emotional response to that sensation, reacting to it, and self-awareness, reflecting on its affect.

As soft-boundaried creatures, the less we have in the brain of processed proprioceptive messages, the more we seek self-confirmation through self-stimulation, not only physical but psychological, reaching out beyond our immediate space for psychological reassurance. We need to know we exist as an entity. We not only learn what we are doing from this comprehensive package, we learn what our boundaries are, what is 'me' and what 'not me' is. We get a sense not only of what we are doing but also the physical and psychological component of who we are – which brings us to the verge of self-awareness.

But suppose that during development, the glial cells in the brain have over-pruned the synaptic connections between the nerve cells (so that incoming stimuli are not arriving at the correct processing networks for their particular sense), or under-pruned these links (so that messages are being drowned by over-firing of the Purkinje cells), the child or adult's initiatives will not be receiving satisfactory confirmation and embodiment. This will have a physical knock-on effect on the growth of the sense of self, which is precisely what so many people on the spectrum are struggling with. All sorts of distortions creep in.

Deriving from both physical and psychological confirmation, it is so easy to lose this fragile sense of 'who I am'. But the sensory problems of the child with autism are compounded by society in that, in order to be seen to behave 'acceptably', they are always getting things wrong and constantly being redirected; particularly, they are not allowed to express how they feel. So if a child says 'I want to hit you', they are either ignored, or reprimanded or restrained. On the other hand, if we reply, 'You really sound as if you want to hit me', we validate how they feel, that the feeling they have is real, it is a part of 'who' they are. On hearing this, in my experience, they will almost always respond, 'oh yes I do' – but it is like opening the valve on a pressure cooker, their voice warms and their body language relaxes immediately. Now someone has acknowledged how they feel they can move on. They know that their feeling is real and it confirms their sense of self. And the crisis does not go any further.

For example, an autistic child comes in late to a session at the day centre where the group is making pancakes. She is told it is too late for her to start. She folds her arms and says, 'Well, if I'm not making pancakes, no-one is going to make pancakes'. Mayhem is about to break out. My colleague takes her to one side and says, 'You really sound as if you want to make pancakes'. The child relaxes at once, breaths out, 'oh yes I do'. But the crisis is over, tension gone[137].

Remembering that autistic people frequently feel miserable, even if they say, 'F*** off', rather than redirecting them to a socially acceptable way of saying, 'go away', which does not acknowledge how they feel, we say, 'you must feel really f****d off', then they will stop, relax and move on. We have to validate these negative feelings in order to help them understand their feelings are real, so they can learn to trust themselves.

At the most extreme level, a child said, 'I want to kill myself'. My colleague met her desolation with, 'You really sound as if you want to kill yourself'. The outcome was the same, 'oh yes, I do', but again, what she needed to know was that someone had heard her despair, and that what she was feeling was a real part of her. Once acknowledged, her pain dispersed[138].

Turning now to those of us who are not on the autistic spectrum; what are these emotions that are so painful that we may decide (at an unconscious level) that they are too hot to handle, red alerts straight off the amygdala, blast with no shield to crouch behind. We may say, 'I can't face this', an unconscious decision that prefers (or is forced), to live with suppressed feelings, listening to its echoes and repercussions from the unknown, rather than looking at them directly, leaving us at the mercy of unprocessed reactions which will affect how we respond to allied situations.

We may be overwhelmed by feelings to the point where we are subsumed by them. It is wartime; out of necessity, a young child is left for three hours with (kind) strangers in a new place in a strange country. She turns her back on them and stands by the gate, yelling non-stop until her mother returns. Subsumed in the noise, she has no thoughts. The shape of abandonment fills her senses; she has no access either to the world round her, no self-control. Looking back, the sound of the child who was engulfed by a tidal wave of loss still resonates in the adult's memory. Which part of her can still hear the (now silent) bellow? The feeling is imprinted, even if she cannot hear the sound.

---

137 Personal communication.
138 Personal communication.

More subtle than this total take-over are the emotions that underpin our disposition, whether we are optimistic or take a negative point of view. Today I feel sad for no particular reason. I (metaphorically) stand back and look at the self who has an emotion called sadness. More like floating on the tide than caught up in a tsunami: I ask myself, 'who is this "I" who is feeling sad'? Before it was just a visceral feeling but now I have taken possession of myself, I have agency of my emotion and it is contributing to my sense of self, so that I can begin to own who and what I am. We need to learn to stand back and look at what we are experiencing in such a way that we self-confirm ourselves.

Damasio says, 'The feeling of an emotion is different from having the emotion in the first place…You can have an emotion without necessarily feeling it'[139]. There is a difference between the automatic recognition and response to the perception of a stimulus (reflex) and our emotional response to that stimulus (sentience), that is, being 'aware' of it and reacting to it and 'self-awareness, reflecting on its affect'. These take place in different parts of the brain.

While it is characteristic of humans that we not only feel stimuli that come from outside and the visceral ones that originate internally, we can also reflect on what these sensations mean. So it comes as something of a surprise to learn that it is possible to note a feeling without knowing what it means. This is especially true of autism where there can be a divorce between perception and interpretation: people on the spectrum may receive a stimulus through the sense organs, recognise it as a sensation but still cannot link the sensation with meaning.

Iris Johansson talks about this absence of connection between sensation and interpretation in her vivid description of her autistic childhood:

She felt hungry *'but does not understand that this sensation means she* [sic] *should eat… I was unable to get food if I was hungry and anyway, hunger did not signal to me that food was what I needed… The peeing business worked only now and then. When the feeling of pee-urge arose, I could feel it in my body but I didn't understand it. It wasn't connected to peeing. Little by little I was able to get the thought in my head that when I had this feeling in my body it was time to pee. It took until I was eleven before I understood that the feeling in my body was pee-urge.'[140]*

In addition to failure to interpret physical sensations, she was unable to connect with feelings as emotions which extended to the emotional world of others:

---

139 Damasio interviewed by David Hirschman, July 2, 2010.
140 Johansson I (2012) *A Different Childhood*, p25. Inkwell Productions.

'Nobody grasped that I had no contact with the emotion field that would give me information that other people seemed to have access to. It was not like this field was missing but a bridge was missing, some kind of transfer, some kind of feeling for others. The peculiar thing about my condition is that there is so often emptiness, a standing still, no impulse whatever, and even though I can see everything and understand everything around me it doesn't give me any impulses for action. It's like being in an invisible glass box.'[141]

Like those of us not on the spectrum, there is a wide variety of reactions to the feelings of affect among people on the spectrum, many of whom have very severe problems with emotions. Those of us who do not share these difficulties to the same extent are inclined to feel that those with autism do not have the ability to emote, but in some cases it is that autistic people are oversensitive to the feelings launched by their sympathetic nervous system; they are too painful, so they have learned to bury them. This situation is brilliantly expressed by Izaak, a man with Asperger's syndrome. He explains that if he is feeling overloaded at college and can't face going to a class, he can only feel it is 'bad'; he cannot argue himself out of it by saying to himself, 'I was really upset at the time and it would have been worse if I had gone in regardless'. For him, he can only think of things in terms of absolutes: 'I can do binary, 1 or 0, good or bad, nothing in between'.

This points towards focusing on valency[142] (what is good for me or bad for me), rather than dwelling on the quality of the experience, since dwelling on affective qualia can trigger overwhelming feelings so powerful that it feels as if the individual is in mortal danger. It can also suggest there may be an absence of connections to the cerebral cortex which would allow him to moderate the painful spike in his autonomic responses. Izaak adds a final explanation, as to how he feels: 'Emotions are like algebra, except you aren't given any of the values'[143].

At the other end of the scale, an autistic person may be swept away by gusts of emotion, where the sympathetic nervous system is described as 'blowing its fuses'. Instead of feeling pleasure in response to emotional warmth, the child or adult feels they are being attacked and responds violently to defend themselves from what presents to them as a life-threatening assault. For these individuals, praise evokes a tsunami of pain. It can be heart-rending for parents desperate to show their child how much they love them, to be met with a wall of rejection.

It is difficult to boost a person's morale and sense of themselves if affection and praise trigger painful surges in the sympathetic nervous system. It also presents

141 Johansson I (2012) *A Different Childhood*, p25. Inkwell Productions.
142 Feinberg E & Mallatt JM (2016) *The Ancient Origins of Consciousness*. Massachusetts: The MIT Press.
143 Izaak. Private communication.

problems to teachers, since it undermines the whole basis of encouraging good work through praise. Richard McGuire who is himself on the spectrum, suggests an oblique approach may be acceptable without triggering emotional overload. Rather than using a direct phrase such as, 'good work', try, 'that seems to have gone well'. If a child is responding negatively to emotional warmth, one way to demonstrate it is by withholding overt expressions of affection. Then they will learn to trust that what you are going to do or say will not trigger painful sensations.

Chapter 13:
Practice: Responsive Communication

One of my working problems is the tendency to fragment different approaches into exclusive specialisms. So the people we are trying to reach receive inputs from many different professions; occupational therapy, music and drama therapies, physiotherapy, speech and language therapy, not to speak of behavioural inputs and Intensive Interaction practitioners: all dedicated to their own particular approaches – the practice of which is scattered over overcrowded timetables and buried in reports.

Put simply, during forty years of using Intensive Interaction to get in touch with people who find language a struggle (both to understand it and to articulate), it has become apparent that my efforts may be hopelessly counterproductive if I am wearing a bright coloured shirt, use a harsh voice, or ignore restless body language when I introduce myself. We can, all of us, tune in much more quickly if we pool our skills and attend to sensory deficits first.

So how can we help people who are struggling with sensory confusion to make sense of the world we share? While I am reluctant to introduce the idea of yet another 'therapy', I do so because our current isolated interventions are leaving a gaping hole in practice: not only is it that what we are offering may not be interpreted in the manner we intend it, but also the environment itself (in its broadest sense) may be contributing to the anxiety of our conversation partners and increasing the difficulty they have in processing our efforts to engage with them.

This chapter focuses on practice. The first part looks at how we can decrease, as far as possible, those elements in the environment that underlie sensory overload. It looks at the hypersensitivities, particularly those of vision and hearing as well as the problem of low levels of proprioception. It does not address the problems of hypersensitivity to smell and taste, since the only way we have at present of alleviating these is avoidance. (The approach of behavioural conditioning is difficult, takes a long time and adds to the burden of anxiety which can have undesirable side effects.)

In the face of sensory onslaught children and adults with autism are looking for coherence, an autism-friendly environment that has meaning for them. Responsive Communication is an overall approach that combines the reduction of signals that are difficult to process by addressing sensory deficits and thereby reducing anxiety, with an increase in signals that do have meaning, using my conversation partner's utterances, movements and rhythms as a basis for conversation (Intensive Interaction). In practice this is proving to be a powerful combination. It is also helpful for children and adults with severe learning difficulties.

Responsive Communication will work for practitioners from any relevant discipline, facilitating their practice: we learn from their skills and offer our own. This is not unprofessional; there are currently just not enough people skilled in working with severe autism. In particular, many teachers are under-trained (or sometimes not at all when it comes to mainstream schooling). In some cases, those with no experience of autism are simply being left to get on with it. This is partly because teachers in training colleges have not always caught up with recent changes in understanding of autism and those in managerial positions gained their working knowledge before recent research was published. There is a real danger that our approaches are out of date.

We need to share any expertise that reduces anxiety, so that the autistic brain is able to work to its maximum efficacy. We cannot afford to be professionally territorial and ghettoize our skills. I learn from my colleagues in different disciplines and share my skills with them.

Part 1: sensory deficits

To put it simply, the deficits, the hyper and hyposensitivities, are due to wiring problems in the brain and are different in each individual. Neuroscience is making rapid advances in our understanding of detail – the differences in volume and density in parts of the brain, the lack of connections between different regions and the over-connectivity between others[144]. These differences are beginning to be linked with overall behaviour patterns, such as a particular deficit and repetitive behaviour (although these may be a parallel effect rather than derivative). However, current research seems to be less precise about what underlies specific hyper and hypo sensitivities themselves. Why is one person's visual processing sensitive to a particular colour (which can be corrected by a specific filter) when it is a different colour that underpins the hypersensitivity in another autistic person?

---

144 Donovan AP & Basson AM (2017) The neuroanatomy of autism, a developmental perspective. *Journal of Anatomy* **230** (1) 4–15.

Nevertheless, what these individuals have in common is that they are easily sensorily overloaded. Our job is to pick up the clues they offer as to where the deficits lie. In practice this is relatively easy if one is working with body language. Particularly evident are what we call 'the flinches', where a child will recoil away from a sensory input that threatens to overload them (avoidance). Or they will shut down, or become distraught, or aggressive, or self-harm. Instead of trying to contain the behaviour we need to identify the underlying cause[145]. I am therefore going to subdivide this chapter on Responsive Communication. The first half looks at the hyper and hypo-sensitivities; we need to think of these in terms of any stimulus that is going to trigger the body's self-defence system. I say this because current assessment may be too gross, focusing on the stimulus rather than its effect and doesn't always include conditions such as scotopic sensitivity/Irlen syndrome[146] and emotional overload.

A typical intervention will involve watching a child or adult for a short while (sometimes only for a few minutes, since their current behaviour, what they are doing now, is my starting point), and easing myself into the feedback they are using to meet their own sensory needs, the language they are using to talk to themselves. I need to know what is going on at this present moment, in terms of how they feel (as expressed through their body language) and engage with this, whether or not it is positive or negative. I am looking to build up trust through confirmation of what they are doing and how they are doing it, and to validate their affective state. So I respond to them, not as copying but as a response, using the individual's body language to build up an effective conversation. I am monitoring when the child or adult is relaxed and when they tense up. And while we are engaged I am on the lookout for hypersensitive reactions – such as the individual who flinches when they look out of the window into bright daylight which tells me they are hypersensitive to bright light and have scotopic sensitivity or Irlen syndrome[147].

Recently I was asked to visit six-year-old Martin, who is deeply autistic. He is running around from one activity to another, tearing up paper and failing to give eye contact or engage with his parents. It is difficult to persuade him to eat and he also hates going outside. He does not respond to my using his sounds to engage his attention. I try switching on a light bulb which can be controlled by a handset

---

145 Further information on working with sensory deficits will be found in *The Anger Box*, Chapters 3, 4 & 5. Available from Pavilion Publishing & Media.

146 Scotopic sensitivity and Irlen syndrome refer to difficulties in processing incoming visual information. Triggered by bright light, pattern and certain colours, it is not a direct problem with the eye and does not register in normal eye tests.

147 I am grateful to Tina Yates of the Irlen Centre who has been generous in helping me to understand the visual difficulties some children on the autistic spectrum have to struggle with. In return, she now uses body language to establish emotional engagement with children she is testing.

to shine in one of sixteen colours[148]. When I get to the blue light, he drops the cardboard he is trying to rip, comes over, takes my hand, gives both myself and his parents full eye contact and engages my hand in operating the bulb. It is at once clear that he has scotopic sensitivity/Irlen syndrome.

Martin, who had not previously demonstrated sustained interest or the ability to engage in any meaningful activity, quickly learns to operate a complex hand-set to switch on the blue light and turns it to the correct colour when he comes into the room. Tina Yates tells me she had worked with a child with eating problems who was able to overcome these when food was presented on a plate that was the same colour as his preferred colour. So bearing in mind Martin's difficulties with eating and going out, I suggest that his parents obtain a blue plate and blue jacket. Martin's mother says he is doing well with both. One has to presume that for Martin, blue represents a colour in which he is able to achieve some sort of coherent sensory picture of his environment. Finding it user-friendly he is now able to refer to it when he starts to become overloaded.

For those who are unfamiliar with it, the work on Irlen syndrome derives from that on dyslexia, where the letters or numbers move around. It was found that using colour filters to cut out certain frequencies (different in each person), corrected the problem that dyslexic people have with reading. Donna Williams, whose visual environment was constantly pixilating, with 'the bits' on the move, thought they might be useful for her. The effect of the tinted lenses, which filter out the particular frequency that is triggering the visual distortions, was to bring the movement to a halt. Donna describes what happened: 'The whole world went shunt' and she said, 'oh my God, that's what the rest of the world is seeing'. She describes her partner's face as joined together:

'His eyes and nose and mouth were all held together with equal impact, in a single context. Then I noticed his neck and shoulders and torso and legs were also joined, not bit by bit as my eyes moved along but as a whole picture ... I looked around the room and it did not seem so crowded, so overwhelmingly bombarding. The background noise I had heard before, machine sounds in distant rooms, the hum of traffic, the mutter of people talking, were not even apparent. I felt I was swimming with the tide not against it.'[149]

Donna's description of her visual processing before she was wearing her corrective lenses sounds to the uninitiated like looking at a sequence of stills from a movie. While those of us who are familiar with the transformational outcomes that can

---

148 Optimum light bulb. See Appendix II.

149 Excerpt from a letter from Donna Williams to Ann Wright of the Irlen Centre describing what happened when she first put on her tinted lenses.

be achieved through the use of tinted lenses and have no problems with their efficacy, recent SPECT scans should allay doubts that have been expressed in the past about the reality of Irlen syndrome[150]. These compare brain activity in a child doing the same task, wearing and not wearing her tinted lenses. When she is not wearing the corrective tint, her brain is firing randomly, compared with normal processing when she is using them.

Mike's visual problems derived from exposure to intense light rather than being attributable to a particular colour. He describes a similarly transformative experience when he first tries his tinted lenses:

'I have my tinted lenses … I thought everyone's eye sight was the same as mine. When I put them on for the first time I was seriously disorientated but soon adjusted, they've made a massive difference in my eye sight and when I go outside I don't squint my eyes half as much now. I have also noticed a difference at school now with my glasses. I haven't been as anxious about school and my panic attacks are a lot better.'

A few weeks later:

'The glasses have made a brilliant difference and teachers can't keep up with me at school and I have been put on a gifted and talented list since I got the glasses. When I take them off at night I still can't believe how bad my eye sight was.'[151]

Bearing in mind that Mike was a child who could barely read or write, recently he emailed me again. Now four years older, he has had to have his eyes retested, as the required tint changes with ageing:

'Having tested a lot of lenses, I have found a particular pair which started to cause improvement in particular behaviours. Firstly I was able to read in a straight line without any deficits such as shimmering and losing my place. I then revisited these afterwards and started to notice more significant differences, such as a sharp increase in my eye contact, my attention to detail and subtleties in the environment (without just glancing at it until it became distorted), as well as my balance, anxiety and my overall speech. I felt as I looked round the environment I could physically detect the blood flow in the back of my head shift to accommodate for this new way of functioning.'

It is difficult to believe now, but when Mike first tried using Irlen lenses, he was in the slow lane of his special school. He was quickly moved to the talented

---

150 SPECT scans of Irlen syndrome. Irlen Centre, Amen Clinic, Newport Beach, CA, USA. More information in: Irlen H (2010) *The Irlen Revolution*. New York: Square One Publishers.

151 Caldwell P (2014) *The Anger Box*. Brighton: Pavilion Publishers and Media Ltd.

stream, and as he outstripped his teachers, he was subsequently sent to a school for gifted children. He is now at college.

Irlen syndrome can affect the visual experience in all sorts of different ways. A young woman I was asked to see called me 'piggy nose' and was desperate to touch my nose all the time. I did not understand this until I was shown drawings done to prescription by the mother of a different child with the syndrome. The drawing showed her looking at a class of children standing in rows. The centre is a black hole surrounded by a periphery of the class, all with distorted pig-like faces. When she wore her corrective tinted lenses, her vision became typical and she could see all the children with normal faces. The same child could not see anything white or silver. While she could feel the bath water, she could not see the white bath. And her teachers found it difficult to teach her about money, since she could only see copper coins, not the silver[152].

Correction of visual deficits does not cure autism but it does remove what amount to physical hurdles to interpreting surroundings. This comes with a warning; currently, Irlen testing is being offered by various different firms and even opticians, but not all are able to engage with children with autism. It is sensible to contact the Irlen Centre who will direct you to trained consultants in your area who understand the nature of autism.

Turning now to auditory hypersensitivity; many autistic children are being bombarded by sound; sometimes painful frequencies or harsh tones, sometimes by overlapping speech which they cannot interpret. Or they can be frightened by sudden noises and particular sounds such as dogs barking or someone coughing, not only when they happen but in anticipation that they may be going to happen. These can be agonising to the point where the child self-harms, for example, by banging their heads, or biting their arms. While we are cautioned that earmuffs may cut out so much auditory stimulus that the child stops listening, they can be helped by using BOSE acoustic noise reduction headphones[153] which are designed so that helicopter pilots can hear each other over the engine noise. These are selective and background noise is reduced by 80%, leaving the child free to hear close-up conversation. They do not stop listening since they can now hear what they wanted to hear in the first place.

Moira is ten. While she has not received an official autism diagnosis, some of her behaviour suggests she has difficulty filtering out important sounds and may well be on the spectrum; in order to be able to focus on her homework, she builds a cave under the table and surrounds it with a sofa and armchairs

---

152 Personal communication through Tina Yates at the Irlen Centre.
153 See Appendix II.

to cut down on overwhelming stimuli. I lend her some BOSE headphones. She writes me a letter:

'Normally in class I can hear everything, others whispering, noise outside, people tapping pencils and dropping them. It's hard to hear the teacher's voice unless she shouts which isn't often. With the earphones, I couldn't hear anything that disrupted me. I wrote more than usual and I could concentrate on learning and could listen to the teacher. I took them off and I was astonished at how different it was.'

Her teachers say that in half an hour, the standard of her work shot up. They said they had not realised, no-one had told them.

Andrew's parents write thanking me for the loan of a pair of headphones:

'We only had an hour to try them on the first day but there was an immediate effect. He got much calmer and never took them off. Next day he wore them all day. He never took them off although they fell off to his shoulders when he was running about. He put them back on. He was less argumentative and seemed more relaxed. He said he felt more comfortable with them on.'

Nye's mother writes:

'I bought some headphones for Nye but never managed to get them on him as he hated wearing things on his head. I've tried them again recently, and he is tolerating wearing them and they have made a huge difference to his ability to cope with his hyper sensitivities. School are amazed too.'

David's mother also found that while her son rejected wearing headphones at first, when she took him into the city where he was exposed to considerable noise, (bagpipes, a generator and trains in the station), he was asking her for them after an hour or so.

We come now to proprioceptive difficulties, which we have already looked at in some detail, with the suggestion that it may not be that the proprioceptive messages are lacking but rather, these are being drowned out by anxiety. Children who are hyposensitive to proprioception actively seek to remediate this by giving themselves powerful pressure stimuli in one way or another. Sometimes the pressure feedback they are giving themselves can be very minimal, as with a small boy I was asked to visit. When the front door opened he was not wearing shoes but stood on the threshold, rubbing his foot backwards and forwards over the doorframe. So I knew before I got into the house that pressure had meaning for him. As he lay on his stomach on the floor, I applied pressure to his back and he responded immediately.

Other children or adults who are low on proprioceptive stimuli crave pressure and will run, jump, climb, hit or bite themselves but also, since proprioception and balance signals are intimately linked, will look for activities that give themselves regular jolts, such as the swing or trampoline, even a pogo stick[154]. What is important is that inputs to meet their needs should be regular and frequent, occasional visits to the trampoline are not enough to meet the deficit.

Pressure garments can help the problem of a lack of sense of boundary. Joe said that a pressure vest stopped his body feeling that it was 'actively blowing itself apart'. Hope tells me that when she is wearing hers, 'it reduces the feeling of being invaded'.

Particularly helpful is a specially designed vest/gilet where the pressure can be adjusted to meet changing anxiety levels at any particular time[155]. For example, a child who finds the stress levels at school difficult to manage leaves home with a low pressure setting; by the end of the day he has pumped it up to full pressure.

Once we start to attend to sensory deficits, it rapidly becomes clear that we cannot assess the intellectual level of children without addressing their sensory needs. But this still leaves us with the problem of lack of social engagement. How can I create an environment that encourages the child or adult to want to be with people?[156]

Part 2: using body language: Intensive Interaction

Body language reflects how we feel, for example we are likely to reflect anxiety through tension in our body posture, facial expressions, voice and level of activity. Intensive Interaction focuses on reading the body language of our conversation partners and responding to what they are doing; particularly how they are doing it, in order to tune in to how they feel. We are looking to promote emotional engagement.

One of the most obvious features of autism is repetitive behaviour; the child or adult is doing something which they focus on and has meaning for them, to the exclusion of a wider range of behaviour. Spiker suggests that repetitive behaviours may be a form of maladaptive coping response to negative affect[157]. (In essence, the more stressed I become, the more I am going try and control my environment.)

---

154 Bluestone J (2005) *The Fabric of Autism*. Redding, CA: The HANDLE Institute.

155 SQUEASE Vest, see Appendix II.

156 Penny Mytton talking to Olly. Caldwell P (2006) *Autism and Intensive Interaction*. London: Jessica Kingsley Publishers. DVD.

157 Spiker MA, Lin CE, Van Dyke M & Wood JJ (2012) Restricted interests and anxiety in children with autism. *Autism* **16** (3) 306–320.

Attention to sensory deficits and using body language to communicate complement each other; both together (i.e. Responsive Communication) can lead to dramatic changes, not only for the individual but for their families and those who teach, support or otherwise engage with them. But what is critical is that once we have reduced the sensory overload (and they are no longer having to struggle with overwhelming anxiety), we can engage with each other as people. As mutual trust grows we can learn to value and respect the individual, not just in terms of behavioural support but as the unique person that they are.

So, if we have used Responsive Communication and reduced the signals that are triggering sensory overload and attendant stress as far as possible, we are now in a position to see body language without the overlay of anxiety. What we are left with is feedback that is hardwired and meaningful and will form the basis for interaction. What we are going to do is to respond to the person's feelings, developing a conversation between us as expressed through their movements and sounds and gestures and rhythms. We are going to confirm how they feel.

The part played in Responsive Communication by Intensive Interaction is not just for the non-verbal. When it comes to engaging with people on the Aspergers end of the spectrum, confirmation of their physical and affective state is just as important as for the less able. Where is their anxiety focused?

Since they are also experiencing sensory chaos, they may retreat or try and control it by establishing a rigid control on their slippery environment and sometimes the people with whom they live. But tackling the problem is the same; reducing the sensory overload and engaging with them through their interests. Can we involve them in arranging an environment where their talents (which may be considerable) will be valued by society? But in particular we need to confirm and validate how they feel as expressed through their speech, so their sense of self is not lost in a limbo of sensory confusion and psychological rejection. The mother of an autistic family who were struggling describes the way that positive support has enhanced her family's quality of life and self-respect. In reference to boundaries, she adds in an interesting comment that her son, 'now feels comfortable in his skin'. In the midst of turmoil, the autistic children and adults need to be able to answer the question, 'Who am I?' with confidence. They need to be rooted in a sensorily rootless environment.

Part 3: confirmation

So what is it about imitation and particularly response to a person's body language that is so effective in luring autistic children and adults out of their inner world, grabbing hold of their attention and helping us to tune into how they feel and to get alongside each other? Because it is not just a one-way intervention, it happens to both of us; we are caught up in the flow of each other's intention. We confirm each other.

Much of what the non-autistic world offers to the autistic is scrambled even before it reaches the processing centres. What they are getting is a garbled version of the world they inhabit. They have little to hang on to. So recognition is central to the process of confirmation; the stimulus they are receiving has to have meaning in the sense of being delivered in an intelligible form, in a language they understand. We need to think carefully about how we deliver information if we want our autistic conversation partner to make sense of it. Bearing in mind their sensory profile, what is it that has significance for this particular person's brain?

Earlier we looked at the dyadic conversation (the intimate conversation between mother and infant), where the infant's initiatives are confirmed by the mother and how the earliest recognisable sense is that of rhythm. Our responses to pressure and sound are intimately linked. Just sixteen weeks after the sperm has burrowed its way into the egg and the fertilised egg has implanted itself into the comfort of the lining of the womb, we have already become sentient, aware of external (to us) stimuli. Pattern recognition starts here before our ears are ready to hear the mother's heartbeat. If our mother is breathing steadily our foetal heartbeat synchronises with hers, to the extent that asynchrony is taken as a sign of foetal distress. If all is going well our hearts beat as one. Even at this early stage, we begin to react to environmental pressure through the amniotic fluid in the form of pressure and of sound. Intonation, patterns of pitch, stress and rhythm are being perceived as alterations in pressure waves which are felt through the skin and skeletal systems[158]. If this is so, proprioceptive reception of prosody precedes hearing through the ears, since although the neonate reacts to sound at this stage, the ear is not fully functional until twenty four weeks. Before the ear can hear, we tune into rhythm at this stage. This is eight weeks before hearing is possible. And the foetus is particularly responsive to the mother's voice[159].

This is some weeks before hearing. So at first in the embryo, sound is being perceived as pattern and change. What interests me is how basic and intertwined with sound reception this pattern recognition can remain in our lives. If we define pattern recognition as 'a cognitive process that matches information from

---

158 Graven SN & Browne JV (2008) Auditory development in the foetus and new-born infant. *Newborn and Infant Nursing Reviews* **8** (4) 187–193.

159 Shahhiddulah S & Hepper PG (1992) Hearing in the foetus. *International Journal of Prenatal and Perinatal Studies* **4** (3/4) 235–240.

a stimulus with information retrieved from the memory'[160], the match does not necessarily have to be exact; it can be 'near enough', 'part of'.

When we are trying to engage children or adults whose brains are not able to make sensory connections easily, it is sometimes possible to get through by offering fragments of the whole in a different mode. What we are looking for is a clue that will trigger recognition. In order to do this it will have to be sufficiently part of the template but not necessarily the whole pattern. It is the slight difference that jogs the brain into recognition with interest.

Patel is 10 years old. He has two different behaviours. Most of the time he wanders around without apparent purpose; his arms and hands flutter randomly, not as in repetitive behaviour, or as in spasm. He does not appear to be in control of his movements at all. He has little eye contact and does not respond when I try engaging with him by using his sounds or movements. I am at a loss as to how to engage with him. But every now and then his behaviour changes; he stops his random movements and moves his head purposefully up and down several times and then swaps over to a different movement, from side-to-side. During this period, Patel appears to be completely in charge of his movements. He knows what he is doing.

So I stand behind him, asking myself what it is that has meaning for him. Perhaps it is simply the pattern of a movement he feels inside himself. Keeping my own head still, when he moves his head vertically, I make the same movement by rubbing my hand up and down on his back. Then he quite deliberately changes to a sideways movement. At once, I change the direction of my rubbing, to and fro, to and fro. Patel relaxes and turns round to me and gives me good eye contact. He has recognised the pattern of feedback I am putting in and appears to be completely calm both then and for twenty minutes afterwards.

What has happened? The change in his behaviour is contingent upon his recognition of a pattern that has meaning for his brain. This is when he is in control of himself (as opposed to when he is wandering round making random movements). But he clearly recognises when 'his pattern' comes from outside himself and his attention shifts to the external source. His response is to a 'good enough' match to his proprioceptive template, physical on physical. I am feeding in to the feeling he is giving himself.

However we may be able to use a completely different mode which nevertheless has enough of the template to be recognisable. I do this when I physically tap out the underlying rhythm of sounds so they are felt rather than heard.

---

160 http://en.wikipedia.org/wiki/Pattern_recognition_(psychology)

Returning to Pranve from Chapters 2 and 8, he bends his head down to watch when I tap the rhythm of 'Where's Charlene' (tap-tap-tap) on his arm. He picks up the relationship between his utterance and my physical response to its rhythm immediately and then tests the system. ('I know she will respond to that rhythm, how about a different one?'). So he comes back with a repeated sound, 'aa-ahh – aa-ahh – aa-ahh' and refers back to me to see what I will make of it. He is pleased when, instead of tapping, I draw a wavy line that relates to his sound on his arm. Now he knows that we have a communication system that works; his new offering is met with a contingent response. He is in connection with the world outside in a way that does not make stressful demands on his processing system. Sometimes the relief expressed by change in body language when a person realises that they have made this connection is as palpable as if they had cracked the Enigma code, which in a sense they have; now they have a way of expressing how they feel and being understood.

Nicky is seeking physical stimuli. He is highly active, literally always on the move, running from one room to another. He enjoys pressure and likes to jump. He takes off his shoes in order to feel the ground. He gives minimal eye contact and is uninterested when I answer his sounds. It occurs to me that there might be an alternative way of giving him a response that has meaning for him by using pressure to respond to him. I ask his father for a belt – he produces a strip of neoprene (this is ideal since when it is pulled the plastic tightens and gives pressure).

Nicky's mother holds him between her knees, facing away from her and wraps the belt round his stomach. Every time Nicky makes a sound she responds in kind but also pulls on the ends of the belt, so he is getting a contingent tug. The effect is instant. He wriggles round so that he is now facing her and becomes highly attentive to her, looking and smiling at her face with good eye contact. Eventually, he points to her mouth and places his finger on her lips.

I am told that Nicky has had glue ear, although this has recently been attended to and is better. It seems possible that, even if he has previously been hearing responses to his sounds, he has not learned to listen to these and link them with his own; he has not realised he can use these to communicate. Up until now his attention has been focused on his overwhelming proprioceptive need which tells him what he is doing.

It is spelling out the pattern of the rhythm of Nicky's utterances that tells him that the contingent sounds made by his mother are related. He begins to understand give and take, the relationship between 'call and response', which he indicates so movingly by reaching out to her, touching her lips. This is an interaction of intimate attention which so graphically illustrates what we mean by emotional engagement.

As already pointed out, our ability to sense through proprioception starts in the womb. It allows us to know our position even if we are in a dark room and cannot see ourselves. Each muscle has a spindle which expands and contracts as the muscle relaxes or tightens and sends a message to the brain[161]. Collectively these messages inform the brain and the brain recognises the pattern of our current position in space, which is of course constantly changing.

When we do learn to communicate, we do not need to have seen a gesture in order to use it to accompany speech. Research into the use of gesture in both congenitally blind and in sighted Turkish and English speakers suggests that even those who have never witnessed the use of gesture employ the same gestures that are typical of their particular language[162]. The patterns of gesture would appear to be hard-wired, even if independent of sight. In other words the links between rhythm, movement and language are fundamental. The gestures that are used are part and parcel of the user's particular language, irrespective or not of whether they have ever been witnessed.

We begin to perceive other than ourselves, the 'not-me', by tuning into rhythms that come from outside ourselves. While channels of speech and visual communication may be scrambled, even people with very severe autism normally recognise the underlying rhythms of their utterances and actions, so that we can offer confirmation even to those who recognise little else.

I want to move on now to other situations where we have been able to use empathetic confirmation specifically to reduce distress.

Richard is desperate to get into the kitchen and gain access to food. Almost as soon as he has finished one chopped apple, he tugs at his mother to open the gate and let him through. If his mother refuses, he goes into complete meltdown, lying on the floor and bellowing. His face is distraught. I suggest that his mother use emphatic gesture, swiping her downward facing hand across her body to accompany the word, 'No' – and sits on the sofa with her arms folded so that he cannot pull her hands. When he recognises that he is not going to get what he wants, he starts bellowing, I show her how to respond to each of his sounds, empathising with his plight. His cries soften as he hears a response that tunes

---

161 Sahyouni (2013) *Proprioception and kinesthesia: Processing the environment.* Khan Academy. Available at: https://www.youtube.com/watch?v=yKfpBGicqNQ (accessed September 2017).

162 Ozcaliskan S (2016) *Seeing Isn't Required to Gesture like a Native Speaker* [online]. Association for Psychological Science. Available at: https://www.psychologicalscience.org/indexphp/news/releases/seeing-isnt-required-to-gesture-like-a-native-speaker.html (accessed September 2017).

in to his misery. We are confirming how he feels. In a few minutes he not only becomes quiet but his body language completely relaxes. He sits there looking at us and eventually gets up and does not go back to his demands. We continue to respond each time he makes a (now soft) sound.

In an attempt to increase the amount of proprioception that does get through to Richard's processing system, I ask his mother to put him on the trampoline at regular intervals. He is also supplied with a tyre on castors and enjoys pushing himself around. (This is good exercise and also has the added bonus that his older sister uses it to play with him.) Feedback informs me that he is calmer and less insistent on breaking into the kitchen. His mother is giving him regular exercise on the trampoline and non-verbal feedback when he makes sounds. These sensations have meaning for him. His mother has also been able to calm him when he is getting upset by responding to his bellows empathetically. But she later reports that he does not have meltdowns so frequently now and is smearing less.

Rosie also has a fixation with food, but in her case it is with rice, not to eat but to play with, dribbling it through her fingers (uncooked). It is the proprioceptive sensation that tells her what she is doing. It feels good and she knows what she is doing when she plays with it. It helps her to keep on track. Periodically she becomes desperate to and tries to climb up on the unit where it is kept on top, out of her way. If access is denied, she ends up on the floor screaming. This is more than a temper-tantrum. Because she is becoming confused, in the midst of chaos she needs the feel of the rice to confirm what she is doing and stave off the meltdown. When I answer her sounds with empathy, she looks up with an expression of surprise. ('That's my sound – or near enough and it's coming from outside me'.) Her attention is shifted from her inner distress to the world outside. She calms down quickly. I show her mother how she can use her fixation to set up a game that involves them both. Instead of her being locked in her inner turmoil and spilling all over the floor, they can now play a mutual game. It may seem a small achievement but Rosie starts to be interested in sharing things, pouring the rice from her plate onto her mother's.

A similar intervention, in the extremely distressed behaviour of a young boy, is recorded in *The Anger Box*[163]. Alister becomes overloaded when circumstances prevent his carrying out a task he has been taught. He does not have the flexibility to deal with an altered context. Conflicting instructions fire his sympathetic nervous system with its pain, confusion and heat. He cannot break out of his anguish until I respond to his bellows with empathy, redirecting his attention to the world outside.

---

163 Caldwell P (2014) *The Anger Box*, p. 5. Brighton: Pavilion Publishing and Media Ltd

In practice, somehow we have to break the perseverant cycle of autonomic distress signals being fired off by the brain. Our response to the person's sensory turmoil shifts their attention away from their own desolation onto ourselves. In order for this approach to be affective, I have to place myself in their mindset. (They will quickly spot if my empathy is not genuine and respond negatively or not at all. I have to genuinely care how they feel, not just make sympathetic sounds.)

Nevertheless, this technique is normally effective, calming a child or adult within minutes rather than an hour or so. It is my first choice when responding to an autonomic storm. Once they are calm, I need to address the sensory trigger that underlies the outburst. They have been terrified and I need to see if I can reduce whatever circumstances set off their distress.

Donna Williams says such fragmentation is like death coming to get her. A child tells us that his head is running away, another that it is like having his head in a car crusher and a third; that it is like having a great black hood coming down over him. This latter description does resemble that offered by the young woman describing her 'shut-down', where her vision shrunk like the point of light on an old-fashioned television set. Everything closes down.

One can only speculate about the attentional shift that accompanies the change from total distress, to interest in the world outside. And when we offer some recognisable fragment, do place cells swing into action, shifting focus and relocating the sense of self from inner turmoil to recognisable ground outside, telling the person that they do exist? Is this what confirmation is doing?

But even if messages have arrived at the brain intact, processing the information is a complex business. It may appear to those of us not on the spectrum to be instantaneous; seeing, recognising and acting on being part of a smooth continuous flow. However it now appears that, at least in the case of self-injury, there is a measurable interval (time to gear up an appropriate response) between a sensorily perceived trigger and its negative self-harming behaviour. Using specially designed mittens to measure the sweat levels on the palms of the hands (a measure of the activity of the sympathetic nervous system) Chris Oliver and his team at Cerebra[164] have demonstrated a consistent ten second lag between the pain stimulus and the onset of self injury. Charley's behaviour illustrates this very clearly.

Charley is ten. Although he can hear, he has very little sight. He also has a whole list of disabilities, including an absence of the corpus callosum, the band of fibres joining the right and left halves of the brain. As pointed out earlier, this condition makes it difficult to link a perceived need with its consequences. Charley's left

---

164 Oliver C (2015) Presentation to the Annual Conference of The Royal College of Psychiatrists.

brain interpreter does not receive physically the messages that would allow it to make up an acceptable and coherent story when his wishes are frustrated. So if Charley wants something (and since he lacks speech he cannot tell us what it is), he becomes extremely anxious – and when he gets anxious he self-injures, banging his head on the table. But before he does this, he bends down and positions his head carefully sideways on the table top. It is clear that he knows what is coming; that he is about to experience an autonomic storm with all its painful effects. But he waits for a few seconds before he starts to crash his head down hard.

As soon as I see him put his head on the table, I intervene, banging the forthcoming rhythm of his self-injury on the wall, interrupting his negative neural build-up. Instead of going into his self-injury, he breaks off, looks up, laughs and walks away. I call this process 'anticipatory confirmation' and we will come back to this later. For the present, two things are necessary to carry off such an approach successfully. The first is that we must be sufficiently familiar with the child or adult's body language to know how the anxiety-self-injury sequence plays out. Secondly, we have to move in immediately they show signs of forthcoming distress. We have not got much time.

But I want to suggest that, in people on the spectrum, such a delay is probably not only true of the build up to self-injury but also true of outwardly directed aggressive responses, when the sympathetic nervous system first starts to respond to a trigger.

So often there is a sequence: first comes the trigger; some form of sensory overload to which the child's sensory problems make them especially vulnerable; an immediate trigger or the outcome of a slow build-up. Either way, the brain cannot process the incoming stimuli fast enough (or it is directed to the 'wrong' processing circuits, or never reaches the appropriate area). Secondly the brain activates the autonomic nervous system, the part of our nervous system that responds to perceived (or real) threat. This has two parts, the parasympathetic nervous system, which slows the body systems down (as in shut-down), and the sympathetic nervous which speeds systems up. The latter is the more common reaction, signified by a change in colour (or acceleration of a repetitive behaviour or some sort of twitch), as the child or adult struggles to maintain some sort grasp on meaning. Care staff will say, 'you can see when she is getting upset, her face changes colour'. The child may flush or go pale, or the mother of a black child tells me that his skin colour changes from ebony to matt black. These behavioural and colour changes are extremely important, as they give us warning of the approaching autonomic storm. It is during this build up of anxiety that we can often intervene successfully, switching focus out of the impending neuronal turmoil by externally anticipating the later stages of the build-up.

In Charley's case I used the rhythm of his anticipated self-injury. But Nye's aggression is directed outside himself. Since he cannot bear the sound of his brother coughing he attacks him when he starts to cough. His mother speaks of a short delay between his brother coughing and Nye attacking him. I asked her to squeeze his hand and make an empathetic sound when she hears his brother cough. He did pinch her but then looked puzzled and did not pursue the attack.

Sandra normally has a cheerful disposition but will suddenly attack staff, pinching their arms severely. This is how she indicates her distress, particularly at noise. Further enquiry suggests that before she pinches she makes a characteristic swift twitch of her head – so there is some warning, even if it is slight. I suggest that if they spot this, they go over to her, and grasp her arm firmly and squeeze, firm enough to be felt but not to hurt her – and then back off. When they tried this anticipatory confirmation, she laughed and did not persist. (At the same time it is important to try and reduce the noise that is upsetting her, in this case the radio which her co-resident enjoys, either by moving her into quieter accommodation or trying headphones – see Appendix II).

Attention to sensory deficits and using body language complement each other; using both together (Responsive Communication) can lead to dramatic changes, not only for the individual but for their families and those who teach, support or otherwise engage with them. But what is critical is that once we have reduced the sensory overload (and they are no longer having to struggle with overwhelming anxiety), we can engage with each other as people. As mutual trust grows we can learn to value and respect the individual, not just in terms of behavioural support, but as the unique person that they are.

Whether or not we are autistic, we all need confirmation, it physically allows us to embody both our physical and psychological experience and strengthens our sometimes precarious sense of self.

Following the Q&A at a recent presentation at the Wellcome Institute, a doctor commented that he had always been taught to think of autism in terms of social isolation and yet here I was talking about intimacy. Which raises the question as to how this can come about, is possible, when so many of the people with whom we engage are emotionally hypersensitive? How is it that we can relate to each other at such a deep level, when closeness can trigger feelings of threat and danger? And in this respect, what do we mean by intimacy?

Intimacy does not necessarily necessitate physical closeness; the sense in which I am using it refers to Winnicott's 'potential space'[165]. the shared psychological

---

165 Winnicott DW (1971) *Playing and Reality*. Hove: Psychology Press.

closeness and bonding of an affective relationship which emerges between mother and child within the dyadic model, particularly in respect of confirmation and growth; an area of bonded relationship that is neither inside or outside but one which emerges as two (child or adult) people probe each other's affective state. It rests on trust and respect.

Unlike our physical boundaries, which are finite, our psychological boundaries are negotiable; like sea-anemones, we test the sentient waters of this shared undermind with myriad feelers; 'me' learns and understands what is important to 'not me'[166]. As we explore what has meaning for each other, we embrace the flow; we learn to respond to positive perceptions and respect those which are negative. We are building a shape, an area which is unique, a place where the most intimate flowering of self is fertilised by profound awareness of other. Here we have no need for defensive boundaries, in trust we just experience being shared in overall being. We become in other.

If this sounds over the top, it is grounded in the particular. Gabriel enjoys swinging a bead on a string. When he does this he knows what he is doing. He is intrigued as I do the same, a response one might dismiss as of trivial importance. But while his attentiveness to me grows from a state of total isolation, on my part I am learning to sense the physical attributes of my actions, about shifting weight, texture, changing colour as the bead catches the light, sensory experiences that I should previously have taken for granted. While I am learning to value the physical attributes of the particular that Gabriel values, in so doing I am conveying my respect for him and his world[167]. And we are having fun together – an interaction that eventually leads Gabriel to the most profound exploration of my face. Eyeball to eyeball, such closeness can be difficult to sustain but it offers both of us a unique experience of both otherness and connection, deepening our experience of what it is to be human.

166 Caldwell P (2016) *Driving South to Inverness*. Brighton: Pavilion Publishing & Media (a biographical exploration of the move into sheltered housing).

167 Caldwell P (2006) *Finding You Finding Me*. London: Jessica Kingsley Publishers and Caldwell P (2010) *Autism and Intensive Interaction*. London: Jessica Kingsley Publishers.

Chapter 14: Conclusion

To sum up, no matter how loving the parental intention, bringing up children with autism can pose a considerable strain on the resources of a family, since the sensory difficulties with which these children are grappling (as they try to interpret what is going on round them) can lead to behaviours which are difficult to contain, let alone with which to develop bonding and engagement. While we have come a long way since 'refrigerator mothers' were being blamed for their children's autism, there can still be an emotional gulf between parents and children which is acutely painful. Mothers will quite often say, 'I do love him but I can't get a response, he just seems to live in his own world and nothing I can do is right. Every now and then he just explodes. I don't know what to do'.

So often families are left stranded by services which are ill equipped to provide the support they need, since the professionals who are managing them were trained before the information that is becoming available now was published. Part of the problem for the families is sheer exhaustion: it is so easy when the child is behaving strangely or in socially embarrassing ways, to shift the blame onto them. We want our children to fit in, to grow up with friends and to find partners; to be happy.

As I have tried to make clear, the problem these children have is in processing incoming information. So we need to reduce the signals that are difficult to process, by addressing sensory deficits, and increasing those that are part of their body language and are easily accessible. Understanding what is going on does help, realising that the child is doing their best and trying to protect themselves from sensory overload and finding ways to work with them rather than just contain behaviours.

It is not only that each child is different; the sheer diversity of autism (which parts of the brain are affected) is part of the problem, so that it is difficult to establish clear rules. However, with the advent of contemporary scanning techniques, neuroscience is changing the way we look at autism; we are moving from broad generalisations into the particularities associated with specific problems.

In this book we have looked not only at the sensory deficits, but, for example, at problems associated with unusual connectivity – and also at damage to the corpus callosum, the belt of fibres joining the two halves of the brain – and how these structural changes might affect behaviour. In simple terms we come back to the young boy who told me his brain was not wired up properly. He seemed quite content with this explanation; it gave him a reason, in terms he understood, as to why he found some things so difficult. But most important of all, we have to remember and respect each individual child and what has meaning for them and to engage with this. We have to learn their language from them. This is a journey we share, and in doing so, we will also learn about ourselves.

Appendix I: Tips on Intensive Interaction

- Intensive Interaction is not something you do *to* a person, it is an interaction that you and they share.

- With each person you have to learn a new language, we are beginners every time.

- Let the person determine proximity. If they show a negative response this is as important as a positive one; back off but do not necessarily break off all contact, just look and see if they are more relaxed.

- Look for the feedback they are giving themselves – this will show you what is significant for them.

- Watch carefully with all your senses, their response may be as little as the flick of an eyelid or a minute sound.

- You have to respond to their initiatives contingently, not necessarily using exactly the same sound, movement, gesture or rhythm, but always one that is part of their conversation repertoire.

- You need to look for how they are making their gestures etc, rather than just what they are doing.

- You have to show them you value what they value.

- Genuine empathy is critical. You have to align yourself with how they are feeling.

- You have to let them lead the conversation, although once you are familiar with your exchanges you can sometimes kick-start the interaction by using an element of their language.

- Enjoy your interaction, have fun with each other.

Appendix II: Sensory deficits toolkit

- **Sensory overload film**
  https://www.youtube.com/watch?v=BPDTEuotHe0
  Film by a woman with autism: 'If you overload the brain it will crash'.

- **Hearing**
  BOSE Quiet Comfort Acoustic Noise Reduction Headphones 15 or 25. The cheapest source is: www.cex.co.uk. There are other brands, we have tried them all and they are not as satisfactory for one reason or another.

- **Vision: Irlen syndrome**
  - Contact Tina Yates at www.irleneast.com to find the nearest Irlen consultant.
  - Coloured light bulb: Optimum LED Colour Changing Bulb (Screw) to find most calming colour, B & M Stores. (Amazon do them also. Do not purchase alternatives.)

- **Proprioception**
  - SQUEASE vest www.squeasewear.com. Available at a reasonable rate for a fortnight's trial. Representative will help fitting etc.
  - Vibration Unit from Boots or Amazon: https://www.amazon.co.uk/Pixnor-P2016-Portable-Cleansing-Massager/dp/B00TKDVFIE/ref=sr_1_4_a_it?ie=UTF8&qid=1472542183&sr=8-4&keywords=facial+massager
  - *Fear of Falling*, a BBC4 film explaining proprioceptive difficulties (fast forward to 50min. if you don't want to watch the foot dissection). Brilliant description of proprioception: http://www.bbc.co.uk/iplayer/episode/p01mv2rj/dissected-2-the-incredible-human-foot
  - Desk bikes: http://www.bbc.com/news/world-us-canada-37420834

- **Loss of sense of self**
  - Ted Talk by Henrik Ehrsson *Illusion of Out-of-body Experience* – currently on YouTube: https://www.youtube.com/watch?v=ee4-grU_6vs

- **Books and contact**
  - See website: www.phoebecaldwell.co.uk

- **More information about Responsive Communication**
  - http://thecaldwellautismfoundation.org.uk/
  - Free training films at the Caldwell Autism Foundation homepage: http://thecaldwellautismfoundation.org.uk/index.php/responsive-communication-the-films/
  - http://thecaldwellautismfoundation.org.uk/

References

Abrams M & Winters D (2013) *Can You See With Your Tongue?* Discover Magazine. Available at: http://discovermagazine.com/2003/jun/feattongue (accessed September 2017).

Baron-Cohen S and Bolton P (1993) *Autism: The facts.* Oxford: Oxford University Press.

Baron Cohen S, Leslie A M & Frith U (1985) Does the autistic child have a theory of mind? *Cognition* **21** 37–46.

Barron J & Barron S (2002) *There's a Boy In There: Emerging from the bonds of autism.* Texas: Future Horizons.

Bauman ML & Kemper TL (2015) *The Neurobiology of Autism* (2nd edition). Baltimore: The John Hopkins University Press.

Berker EA, Berker AH and Smith A (1986) Translation of Broca's 1865 report. Localisation of speech in the third left frontal convolution. *Archives of Neurology* **43** 1065-1072.

Bluestone J (2005) *The Fabric of Autism.* Redding, CA: The HANDLE Institute.

Bolte Taylor J (2009) *My Stroke of Insight: A brain scientist's personal journey.* London: Hodder & Stoughton.

Bolte Taylor J (2008) *My Stroke of Insight.* Ted Talk. Available at: https://www.ted.com/talks/jill_bolte_taylor_s_powerful_stroke_of_insight (accessed September 2017).

Botnik M & Cohen J (1998) Rubber hands 'feel' touch that eyes see. *Nature* **391** (6669) 756.

Caldwell P (2006) *Finding You Finding Me.* London: Jessica Kingsley Publishers.

Caldwell P (2010) *Autism and Intensive Interaction: Using body language to reach children on the autistic spectrum.* Film, Jessica Kingsley Publishers.

Caldwell P (2014) *The Anger Box.* Brighton: Pavilion Publishing & Media Ltd.

Caldwell P (2016) *Driving South to Inverness.* Brighton: Pavilion Publishing & Media.

Caldwell P and Horwood J (2007) *From Isolation to Intimacy.* London: Jessica Kingsley Publishers.

Carswell B. *Andreas Vesalius' Fabrica: The Anatomy of a Revolution.* Available at: https://www.abebooks.com/rare-books/andreas-vesalius-fabrica.shtml (accessed September 2017).

Centers for Disease Control and Prevention (2014) Prevalence of Autism Spectrum Disorder among Children Aged 8 Years – Autism and Developmental Disabilities Monitoring Network, 11 Sites, United States, 2010. *Morbidity and Mortality Weekly Report* **63** (2).

Clarke E and Dewhurst K (1974) *An Illustrated History of Brain Function.* Los Angeles: University of California Press.

Courage KH (2013) Even severed octopus arms have smart moves. *Scientific American* **27** August.

Courchesne E, Karns CM, Davis HR, Ziccardi R, Carper RA, Tigue ZD, Chisum HJ, Moses P, Pierce K, Lord C, Lincoln AJ, Pizzo S, Schreibman L, Haas RH, Akshoomoff NA & Courchesne RY (2001) Unusual brain growth patterns in early life in patients with autistic disorder: an MRI study. *Neurology* **57** (2) 245–254.

Courchesne E, Yeung-Courchesne R, Press GA, Hesselink JR & Jernigan TL (1988) Hypoplasia of cerebellar vermal lobules VI and VII in autism. *New England Journal of Medicine* **318** (21) 1349–1354.

Cytowic RE (2002) *Synesthesia: A union of the senses* (2nd edition). Cambridge, MA: The MIT Press.

Cytowic RE (2003) *The Man Who Tasted Shapes*. Cambridge, MA: MIT Press.

Damasio A (1999) *The Feeling of What Happens: Body and emotion in making of consciousness*. London: William Heinemann.

Deweerdt S (2010) *Connections Between Language Areas Impaired in Autism*. Spectrum News. Available at: https://spectrumnews.org/news/connections-between-language-areas-impaired-inautism/ (accessed September 2017).

DeWeerdt S (2013) *Lack of Corpus Callosum Yields Insights into Autism* [online]. Spectrum News. Available at: https://spectrumnews.org/news/lack-of-corpus-callosum-yields-insights-into-autism/ (accessed September 2017).

Dinstein I, Heeger DJ, Lorenzi L, Minshew NJ, Malach R & Behrmann M (2012) Unreliable evoked responses in autism. *Neuron* **75** (6) 981–991.

Donovan AP & Basson AM (2017) The neuroanatomy of autism, a developmental perspective. *Journal of Anatomy* **230** (1) 4–15.

Du Pui MS (1780) *De Homino Dextro et Sinistro*.

Eagleman D (2015) *The Brain: The story of you*. London: Canongate Books.

Eagleman D (2015) *Can we Create New Senses for Humans?* TED Talk. Available at: https://www.ted.com/talks/david_eagleman_can_we_create_new_senses_for_humans (accessed September 2017).

Feinberg TE and Mallatt M (2016) *The Ancient Origins of Consciousness*. Cambridge, MA: MIT Press.

Fox D (2013) Secret life of the brain. In: J Webb (Ed) *Nothing: Surprising insights everywhere from zero to oblivion*. London: Profile Books Ltd.

Gazzaniga M. *Severed Corpus Callosum*. Available at: www.youtube.com/watch?v=RFgtGIL7vEY (accessed September 2017).

Geschwind N (1970) The organization of language and the brain. *Science* **170** (3961) pp. 940–944.

Grandin T (1992) *A is for Autism film*. Available on YouTube.

Grandin T (2014) *The Autistic Brain*. London: Rider Books.

Graven SN & Browne JV (2008) Auditory development in the foetus and new-born infant. *Newborn and Infant Nursing Reviews* **8** (4) 187–193.

Guterstam A, Biornsdotter M, Gentile G & Ehrsson HH (2015) Posterior cingulate cortex integrates the senses of self-location and body ownership. *Current Biology* **25** (11) 1416–1425.

Haler L, Arnott S & Goodale M (2011) Neural correlates of natural human echolocation in early and late blind echolocation experts. *PLOS One* **6** (5).

Happé F (1994) *Autism: An introduction to psychological theory*. London: University College London Press.

Hood B (2012) *The Self Illusion: How the social brain creates identity*. Oxford: Oxford University Press.

Irlen H (2010) *The Irlen Revolution*. New York: Square One Publishers.

Jeong-Won J, Tiwari VN, Behen HT & Chugani DC (2014) In vivo detection of reduced Purkinje cell fibers with diffusion MRI tractography in children with autistic spectrum disorders [online]. *Frontiers in Human Neuroscience* **8** (110). Available at: http://journal.frontiersin.org/article/10.3389/fnhum.2014.00110/full (accessed September 2017).

Johansson I (2012) *A Different Childhood*. Arizona: Inkwell Productions.

Jolliffe T, Lansdown R & Robinson C (1992) Autism: a personal account. *Communication* **26** 3.

Jones SS (2009) The development of imitation in infancy. Philosophical Transactions of the Royal Society B: *Biological Sciences* **364** (1528) 2325–2335.

Just MA, Cherkassky VL, Keller TA, Kana K & Minshew NJ (2007) Functional and anatomical cortical underconnectivity in autism: evidence from an fMRI study of an executive function task and corpus callosum morphometry. *Cerebral Cortex* **17** (4) 951–961.

Just MA, Cherkassky VL, Keller TA, Minshew NJ (2004) Cortical activation and synchronisation during sentence comprehension in high functioning autism. *Brain* **127** (8) 1811–1821.

Kano M, Wang SS-H & Hansel C (2014) Cerebellar plasticity and motor learning deficits in a copy-number variation mouse model of autism. *Nature Communications* **5** (5586) doi:10.1038/ncomms6586. Available at: https://www.nature.com/articles/ncomms6586 (accessed September 2017).

Kendrick M (2009) *Tasting the Light: Device lets the blind "see" with their tongues*. Scientific American. Available at: www.scientificamerican.com/article/device-lets-blind-see-with-tongues/ (accessed September 2017).

Kerm JK, Geier D, Sykes L & Geier R (2015) Relevance of neuroinflammation and encephalitis in autism. *Frontiers in Cellular Neuroscience* **9** (128) 519.

Kish D (2015) *How I Use Sonar to Navigate the World*. Ted Talk. Available at: https://www.ted.com/talks/daniel_kish_how_i_use_sonar_to_navigate_the_world (accessed September 2017).

Liebermann JA (2015) *Shrinks: The untold story of psychiatry*. London: Weidenfield and Nicolson.

Lokhorst G-JC (1985) Hemisphere differences before 1800. *Behavioural and Brain Sciences* **8** (4) 642.

Loos GH & Loos Miller IM (2004) *Shutdown States and Stress Instability in Autism*. Cuewave Corporation.

Mehrabian A & Ferris SR (1967) Inference of attitudes from nonverbal communication in two channels. *Journal of Consulting Psychology* **31** (3) 248–252.

Minshew NJ and Williams DL (2007) The new neurobiology of autism: cortex, connectivity, and neuronal organization. *Archives of Neurology* **64** (7) 945–950.

Ozcaliskan S (2016) *Seeing Isn't Required to Gesture like a Native Speaker*. Association for Psychological Science. Available at: https://www.psychologicalscience.org/indexphp/news/releases/seeing-isnt-required-to-gesture-like-a-native-speaker.html (accessed September 2017).

Ozonoff S, Pennington BF & Rogers SJ (1991) Executive functioning deficits in high-functioning autistic individuals: relationship to theory of mind. *Journal of Child Psychology and Psychiatry* **32** (7) 1081–1105.

Paul LK, Van Lancker-Sidtis D, Schieffer B, Dietrich R & Brown WS (2003) Communicative deficits in agenesis of the corpus callosum: Nonliteral language and affective prosody *Brain and Language* **85** (2) 313–324.

Pell MD, Rothermich K, Liu P, Paulmann S, Sethi S & Rigoulot S (2015) Preferential decoding of emotion from human non-linguistic vocalisations versus speech prosody. *Biological Psychology* **11** (1) 14–25.

Pierce K, Müller RA, Ambrose J, Allen G, Courchesne E (2001) Face processing takes place outside the fusiform 'face area' in autism: evidence from functional MRI'. *Brain* **124** (10) 2059–2073.

Piochon C, Kloth AD, Grasselli G, Titley HK, Nakayama H, Hashimoto K, Wan V, Simmons DH, Eissa T, Nakatani J, Cherskov A, Miyazaki T, Watanabe M, Takumi T, Purves D, Augustine GJ, Fitzpatrick D, Katz LC, LaMantia A-S, McNamara JO & Williams SM (2001) *Neuroscience* (2nd edition). Sunderland, MA: Sinauer Associates.

Raichle ME, Macleod AM, Snyder AZ, Powers WJ, Gusnard DA & Shulman Gl (2001) A default mode of brain function. *PNAS* **98** (2) 676–682.

Ramachandran VS (2007) *Three Clues to Understanding your Brain*. Ted Talk. Available at: https://www.youtube.com/watch?v=Rl2LwnaUA-k (accessed September 2017).

Rodgers J, Riby DM, Janes EJ, Connolly B & McConachie H (2012) Anxiety and repetitive behaviours in autism spectrum disorders and williams syndrome: a cross-syndrome comparison. *Journal of Autism and Developmental Disorders* **42** (2) 175.

Sadato N, Pascual-Leone A, Grafman J, Ibañez V, Deiber MP, Dold G & Hallett M (1996) Activation of the primary visual cortex by braille reading in blind subjects. *Nature* **380** 6574 526–528.

Sahyouni (2013) *Proprioception and kinesthesia: Processing the environment*. Khan Academy. Available at: https://www.youtube.com/watch?v=yKfpBGicqNQ.

Sandin S, Lichtenstein P, Kuja-Halkola R, Larsson H, Hultman CM & Reichenberg A (2014) The familial risk of autism. *Journal of the American Medical Association* **311** (17) 1770-1777.

Shahhiddulah S & Hepper PG (1992) Hearing in the foetus. *International Journal of Prenatal and Perinatal Studies* **4** (3/4) 235–240.

Spiker MA, Lin CE, Van Dyke M & Wood JJ (2012) Restricted interests and anxiety in children with autism. *Autism* **16** (3) 306–320.

Stern D (1985) *The Interpersonal World of the Infant: A view from psychoanalysis and developmental psychology*. New York: Basic Books Inc.

Stiles A (2012) *Popular Fiction and Brain Science in the Late Nineteenth Century*. Cambridge: Cambridge University Press.

Takashima F and Matsuishi T (2017) *Autism as Seen from the Field of Neuroscience* (paper in preparation). Available at: matsuishi-lab.org/autismunderstanding-brainscienceJP_EN.htm (accessed September 2017).

Tang G, Gudsnuk K, Kuo SH, Cotrina ML, Rosoklija G, Sosunov A, Sonders MS, Kanter E, Castagna C, Yamamoto A, Yue Z, Arancio O, Peterson BS, Champagne F, Dwork AJ, Goldman J, Sulzer D (2014) Loss of mTOR-dependent macroautophagy causes autistic-like synaptic pruning deficits. *Neuron* **83** (5) 1131–1143.

The Boy Who Sees Without Eyes (2007). Extraordinary People documentary series, currently available on YouTube.

Trouvain J (2014) Laughing, breathing and clicking – the prosody of non-verbal vocalisations. *Speech Prosody* 598-602.

Wigan AL (1844) *A New View of Insanity: The duality of the mind*. London: Longman, Brown, Green, and Longmans.

Williams D (1995) *Somebody Somewhere: Breaking Free from the World of Autism*. New York: Broadway Books.

Williams D (1996) *Autism: An Inside Out Approach*. London: Jessica Kingsley Publishers.

Williams D (1996) *Jam-Jar*. Channel 4 programme. Glasgow: Fresh Film and Television.

Williams D (1998) *Nobody Nowhere: The Remarkable Autobiography of an Autistic Girl*. London: Jessica Kingsley Publishers.

Winnicott DW (1971) *Playing and Reality*. Hove: Psychology Press.

Zhan Y, Paolicelli RC, Sforazzini F, Weinhard L, Bolasco G, Pagani F, Vyssotski AL, Bifone A, Gozzi A, Ragozzino D, Gross CT (2014) Deficient neuron-microglia signaling results in impaired functional brain connectivity and social behavior. *Nature Neuroscience* **17** (3) 400–406.

Other titles by Phoebe Caldwell available from Pavilion Publishing

The Anger Box:
Sensory turmoil and pain in autism

Shifting attention away from presentation and symptoms of autism alone, Phoebe explores and attempts to understand the sensory issues experienced by those on the autistic spectrum and their neurobiological roots in an effort to find new ways of alleviating the distress that can characterise adults and children on the autistic spectrum.

Available at: https://www.pavpub.com/the-anger-box/

Creative Conversations:
Communicating with people with profound and multiple learning disabilities (DVD)

This DVD training resource seeks to bridge the gap in the range of currently available material on the use of Intensive Interaction and shows how Intensive Interaction is used to find ways of communicating with people who have multiple and profound learning disabilities, enabling them to express their feelings as well as their needs. It shows care staff and family carers learning to use a number of simple Intensive Interaction techniques with four adults, under the guidance of Phoebe Caldwell. It also includes explanatory discussion between Phoebe Caldwell and Pene Stevens, a clinical nurse specialist in the field, and from the carers themselves supplement these powerful films.

Available at: https://www.pavpub.com/creative-conversations/

Learning The Language:
Building relationships with people with severe learning disability, autistic spectrum disorder and other challenging behaviour (DVD)

Building on Phoebe's previous bestselling books, this DVD resource demonstrates the techniques carers can use to build positive relationships with people with severe learning disabilities and challenging behaviour. Phoebe uses a combined approach of using a person's own 'language' to communicate with them (Intensive Interaction) while also trying to reduce the stress they experience by an exploration of their sensory reality and hyper-sensitivities. The DVD shows Phoebe establishing contact for the first time with a man with severe autistic spectrum disorder; support workers demonstrating how they put the techniques into action in their daily routines, and how new ways of communicating can make a difference to the lives of all concerned.

Available at: https://www.pavpub.com/learning-the-language/

Listening with All Our Senses:
Establishing communication with people on the autism spectrum or those with profound learning disabilities and sometimes distressed behaviour

The three texts brought together in this handbook offer a new perspective for those supporting people with ASD and/or profound and multiple learning disabilities. Phoebe Caldwell emphasises the importance of shifting the focus away from the label of 'challenging behaviour' and instead offers practical advice for ways that we can help to alleviate the distress that may be at the route of such behaviours, by communicating with people on their own terms and in their own 'language'. She uses multiple case studies from her years of experience in the field to illustrate Intensive Interaction and the innovative techniques that she has developed for entering the person's world, as they experience it, and approaching two-way communication from this perspective.

Available at: https://www.pavpub.com/listening-with-all-our-senses/

Delicious Conversations:
Reflections on autism, intimacy and communication

The book deals not only with ways of working in a professional context but also takes a more general look at the nature of affective communication and how we can learn to 'read' other people by recognising our subconscious reactions to their body language.

Caldwell offers practical advice for ways that we can tap into our intuitive minds and share an intimate connection with our communication partners, building a dialogue that does not rely on speech but makes use of all of our senses. Using examples from her own experience Caldwell emphasises that these techniques can help to alleviate the distress that may be at the route of stereotypic behaviours, by communicating with people on their own terms and in their own 'language'.

Available at: https://www.pavpub.com/delicious-conversations/

Driving South to Inverness:
A postscript to an active life

In this thought-provoking memoir Phoebe reflects on her work, childhood and family life and she shares her insights into life, faith, art and philosophy, the opportunities and failings of modernity, and her frustrations with her altered situation as she accepts the changes she faces in old age.

Available at: https://www.pavpub.com/driving-south-to-inverness/

Other useful resources from Pavilion

A Mismatch of Salience:
Explorations of the nature of autism from theory to practice

By Damian Milton

A Mismatch of Salience brings together a range of Damian Milton's writings that span more than a decade. The book explores the communication and understanding difficulties that can create barriers between people on the autism spectrum and neurotypical people. It celebrates diversity in communication styles and human experience by re framing the view that autistic people represent a 'disordered other' not as an impairment, but a two-way mismatch of salience. It also looks at how our current knowledge has been created by non-autistic people on the 'outside', looking in. *A Mismatch of Salience* attempts to redress this balance.

Available at: https://www.pavpub.com/a-mismatch-of-salience/

Choosing Autism Interventions:
A research-based guide

By Bernard Fleming, Elisabeth Hurley and The Goth

This best-selling book provides an accessible evidence-based overview of the most commonly used interventions for children and adults on the autism spectrum. It summarises best clinical practice from the National Institute for Health and Care Excellence (NICE) and gives a set of tools to help you evaluate interventions for yourself. It is the first guide of its kind to meet the requirements of the NHS Information Standard.

Available at: https://www.pavpub.com/choosing-autism-interventions/

10 Rules for Ensuring People with Learning Disabilities and those who are on the Autism Spectrum Develop 'Challenging Behaviour'
...And maybe what we can do about it

By Damian Milton, Richard Mills and Simon Jones

Written in the voice of someone with autism, this pocket sized booklet directly addresses the many practices and assumptions that that cause so many problems for children and adults with autism and learning difficulties and their family, friends and carers.

Available at: https://www.pavpub.com/10-rules-for-challenging-behaviour/

Understanding Autism:
A training pack for support staff and professionals based on 'Postcards from Aspie World'

By Dan Redfearn, Holly Turton, Helen Larder and Hayden Larder

This unique training pack is based on the premise that learning from the experience of someone on the autism spectrum can help those who support individuals to understand and to adapt their approach and therefore achieve better outcomes. Each pack comes with a set of postcards created by a young woman with Asperger's syndrome. The postcards are also available to buy separately and are a valuable resource to prompt and aid discussion.

Available at: https://www.pavpub.com/understanding-autism/

Autism Spectrum Conditions: A guide

by Eddie Chaplin, Steve Hardy and Lisa Underwood

Published in association with the Estia Centre, this guide provides a comprehensive introduction to working with people who have autism spectrum conditions.

Available at: https://www.pavpub.com/autism-spectrum-conditions/

Understanding and Supporting Children and Adults on the Autism Spectrum

by Julie Beadle-Brown and Richard Mills

This unique multi-media training and learning resource, informed by both research and practice, is written by experts and designed not only to help people understand autism spectrum conditions but also to give them a person-centred framework of intervention and support for children or adults on the autism spectrum.

Available at: https://www.pavpub.com/understanding-and-supporting-children-andadults-on-the-autism-spectrum/

Autism Arts Levels 1, 2 & 3

by Abigail Barragry

Autism Arts is a drama syllabus that encourages children who are on the autism spectrum to express themselves, interact and use their imaginations.

Available at: https://www.pavpub.com/autism-arts-level-1/